VINEGAR OF THE FOUR THIEVES

RECIPES & CURIOUS TIPS FROM THE PAST

Follow Donna R. Causey

www.alabamapioneers.com

www.daysgoneby.me

Follow on Facebook at

http://www.facebook.com/ribbonoflove

http://www.facebook.com/alabamapioneers

http://www.facebook.com/daysgonebyme

and

Twitter

http://twitter.com/alabamapioneers

VINEGAR OF THE FOUR THIEVES

RECIPES & CURIOUS TIPS

FROM THE

PAST

COMPILED

BY

DONNA R. CAUSEY

ISBN- 13: 978-1517010201
ISBN-10:1517010209
Soft-cover edition

ASIN: B0054YFC1E
Kindle edition

DEDICATION
This book is dedicated to all
my parents and grandparents

PREFACE

While completing research for my historical fiction series, Tapestry of Love, set in colonial America, and transcribing articles for my websites www.alabamapioneers.com and www.daysgoneby.me, I frequently uncovered interesting information on the daily lives our ancestors.

This book is a compilation of some of the funny and helpful tidbits I discovered in my research.

I've only attempted a few of the hints, tips and/or recipes so I can not vouch for them all. Some recipes date back to 1770s. One or two sound a little dangerous and I would never try them myself, but I've included then in this book for their humorous and historical value. A few are useful, especially for our 'green' society today.

We often reminiscence about the simpler life of the *GOOD OLE DAYS* but after discovering the difficulties our ancestors experienced in daily life, I'm glad I am living today.

Be sure to check out the first two chapters of *Ribbon of Love* – Book One of my Tapestry of Love series at the end of this book.

Donna R. Causey

Table of Contents

With first two chapters of historical fiction novel , Ribbon of Love

PESTS..PESTS...GO AWAY

Pests, such as flies, mosquitoes ants, roaches and etc. were a big problem before the days of chemicals and exterminators. Many people came up with their own personal solutions and some ideas worked quite well.

REPELLING ANTS

- Stop ants in your house by plugging the hole where ants are coming from with petroleum jelly or soft soap.

- Troublesome ants: A heavy chalk mark laid a finger's distance from your sugar box and all around (there must be no space not covered) will surely prevent ants from troubling.

- Surround anthills with used coffee grounds and they will not cross the barrier.

- Repel ants by putting a few drops of clove or peppermint oil on a cloth and wipe counter-tops.

- Red ants can be kept out of the pantry if a small quantity of green sage is placed on shelves.

- A small bay of sulphur kept in a drawer or cupboard will drive away red ants.

REPELLING FLIES

- Sponge your tabletops with white vinegar and water to discourage houseflies from landing.

- The branches of elderbush hung in the dining room will clear the house of flies. There is an odor in them which flies detest.

- To keep flies off, paint wall or rub over picture frames with laurel oil.

- To repel houseflies, sprinkle the kitchen tablecloth with a mixture of 2 tablespoons oil of lavender and 1 cup of rubbing alcohol.

- To keep flies off meat, put meat in sacks, with enough straw around it so the flies cannot reach through. Three-fourths of a yard of yard-wide muslin is the right size for the sack. Put a little straw in the bottom, then put in the ham and lay straw in all around it; tie it tightly and hang it in a cool, dry place. Be sure the straw is all around the meat, so the flies cannot reach through to deposit the eggs. (The sacking must be done early in the season before the fly appears.) Muslin lets the air in and is much better than paper. Thin muslin is as good as thick, and will last for years if washed when laid away when emptied.

- To rid a room of houseflies, put a sponge in a saucer and saturate with oil of lavender. Put on in each room and no flies will stay.

REPELLING MOTHS

- To keep woolens and furs from moths, be sure that none are in the articles when they are put away; then take a piece of strong brown paper, with no holes through which even a pin can enter. Put the article in it with several lumps of gum camphor between the folds; place this in a close box or trunk. Cover every joint with paper. A piece of cotton cloth, if thick and firm, will do the trick. Wherever a knitting-needle can pass, the parent moth can enter.

- Place pieces of camphor, cedar-wood, Russia leather, tobacco-leaves, whole cloves, or anything strongly aromatic, in the drawers or boxes where furs and other things to be preserved from moths are kept and they will never be harmed. Mice never get into drawers or trunks where gum camphor is placed.

- To keep moths out of stored clothing, sprinkle with pepper or tobacco which leaves no unpleasant odor, and can be easily shaken out before wearing.

REPELLING ROACHES, MICE AND OTHER BUGS

- Keep bugs away from your paint by adding a few drops of liquid citronella to the paint.

- A bottle of pennyroyal left uncorked in your bedroom at night will keep the room free of mosquitoes and other insects.

- Dissolve two pounds of alum in three or four quarts of water. Let it remain over night till all the alum is dissolved. Then with a brush, apply boiling hot to every joint or crevice in the closet or shelves where croton bugs, ants, cockroaches, etc., intrude; also to the joints and crevices of bedsteads, as bed bugs dislike it as much as croton bugs, roaches, or ants. Brush all the cracks in the floor and mopboards. Keep it boiling hot while using.

- Borax sprinkled around the doors or on porches will keep bugs out.

- To get rid of roaches, scatter sodium fluoride around their haunts such as dark corners, closets, around water pipes. Use liberally and soon be rid of these pests.

- Molding clay in a mouse trap works fine as a bait and lasts a long time too.

- Place a mirror upright in garden to scare woodchucks away.

- To catch mice, place a gumdrop in the trap, instead of bacon or cheese. When the mouse goes to eat the gumdrop his or her teeth gets stuck and causes the trap to go off.

REMEDIES FOR STINGS AND BITES

- Rub chigger bites with an aspirin tablet, slightly dampened.

- At the first attack of a chigger, let a drop of ammonia touch the affected spot and cure is immediate.

- For Chigger of Mosquito Bites: Use an application of calamine lotion, which can be secured at any drug store.

- A simple remedy which usually kills the chigger after the first application is kerosene oil and table salt, equal parts.

- Bee stings may be quickly remedied by applying repeatedly a soft paste of salertus (baking soda) and water – the potash neutralizes the acid poison.

- The stings of mosquitoes and other similar insects may be relieved by the application of ammonia, or common table salt well rubbed in, or a slice of onion, placed directly to the afflicted part.

MIRROR..MIRROR ON THE WALL

Our ancestors wanted to have beautiful hair and improve body odor so they often came up with their own unique recipes for toiletries. Some of these are included below.

TOILETRIES

- LAVENDER WATER – Oil of lavender two ounces, orris root half an ounce, spirits of wine one pint. Mix and keep two or three weeks. It may then be strained through two thicknesses of blotting-paper and is then ready for use.

- CREAM OF LILIES – Best white castor oil; pour in a little strong solution of sal tatar in water, and shake it until it looks thick and white. Perfume with lavender.

- COLOGNE WATER - (Superior) Oil of lavender two drachms, oil of rosemary one drachm and a half, orange, lemon and bergamot, one drachm each of the oil; also drachms of the essence of musk, attar of rose ten drops, and a pint of proof spirit. Shake all together thoroughly three times a day for a week.

- JOCKEY CLUB BOUQUET - Mix one pint of extract of rose, one pint extract of tuberose, half a pint of extract of cassia, four ounces extract of jasmine, and three ounces tincture of civet. Filter the mixture.

- CREAM OF ROSES – Olive oil one pound, attar of roses fifty drops, oil of rosemary twenty-five drops; mix, and color with alkanet root.

- ROSE-WATER - Preferable to the distilled for a perfume, or for culinary purposes: Attar of rose, twelve drops; rub it up with half an ounce of white sugar and two drachms carbonate magnesia; then add gradually one quart of water and two ounces of proof spirit, and filter through paper.

- BAY RUM – French proof spirit one gallon, extract bay six

ounces. Mix and color with caramel; need no filtering.

CLEANSERS and SALVES

- COLD CREAM – Melt one ounce oil of almonds, half ounce spermaceti, one drachm white wax, and then add two ounces of rose-water, and stir it constantly until cold.

- LIP SALVE – Melt one ounce white wax, one ounce sweet oil, one drachm spermaceti, and throw in a piece of alkanet root to color it, and, when cooling, perfume it with oil rose, and then pour it into small white jars or boxes.

- To help dry skin, add lemon juice or vinegar to your bath water

- Mix drops of rose water with a tablespoon of honey to make a lip balm for chapped lips.

HAIR IMPROVEMENT

- HAIR INVIGORATOR - Bay rum two pints, alcohol one pint, castor oil one ounce, carb. ammonia half an ounce, tincture of cantharides one ounce. Mix well. The compound will promote the growth of the hair and prevent it from falling out.

- MACASSAR OIL FOR THE HAIR - Renowned for the past fifty years, is as follows: Take a quarter of an ounce of chippings of alkanet root, tie this in a bit of coarse muslin and put it in a bottle containing eight ounces of sweet oil; cover it to keep out the dust; let it stand several days; add to this sixty drops of tincture of cantharides, ten drops of oil of rose, neroli and lemon each sixty drops, let it stand one week and you will have one of the most powerful stimulants for the growth of the hair ever known.

- FOR DANDRUFF - Take glycerine four ounces, tincture of cantharides five ounces, bay rum, four ounces, water two ounces. Mix, and apply once a day and rub well down the scalp.

HOW TO AVOID WRINKLES

The following is from a 1903 book The Perfect Woman, on how to avoid wrinkles. I wished it worked.

- "Mme Pote says not even worry will make a woman grow wrinkled and old so rapidly as sleeping with the head upon high pillows. The tendency of the muscles through the day is to droop; this can be counteracted by sleeping on a low pillow."

BALDNESS

This is an excerpt about the reason for Baldness from 1883 Ladies Guide in Health and Disease by Kellogg:

- There are two varieties of baldness, the ordinary form, and what is known as "patchy baldness," a form in which the hair is lost only in circumscribed spots. The loss of hair is usually begins first at the temples, the forehead, or the crown, gradually extending. It is very common in old age, being the result of the general decline in nutrition which occurs in advanced life. When it occurs in early life, it most commonly results from the disease of the scalp known as dandruff.

- Baldness also results from eczema and from ringworm and favus. Temporary baldness not infrequently follows erysipelatous, typhoid and other fevers. Baldness may be occasioned by anything which deteriorates the general health.

- Excessive brain labor causes baldness, resulting in congestion of the head and too much heat in the scalp, may produce it. It may be the result of dyspepsin, of excesses of various kinds, and of any debilitating disease. Men suffer more than women, which is probably due to the fact that women do not habitually overheat the head by the constant wearing of warm head coverings. In some cases, the disease is hereditary.

BEAUTY TIPS (1875-1880)

- An elegant preparation for removing tan is made of one-half pint of new milk mixed with one-quarter ounce lemon juice and one-half ounce of brandy. Bring ingredients to a boil and remove the scum. Use night and morning.

- Some people have moist, clammy hands, very disagreeable to the touch. Exercise, plain living and the local application of starch powder and lemon juice will cure this affliction.

- Warding off wrinkles is prolonged by a simple secret: the tepid bath to which bran is stirred, followed by long friction, till the flesh fairly shines. This keeps the blood at the surface, and has its effect to warding off wrinkles.

- To whiten the arms for an evening party or theatricals, rub them well with glycerine, and before the skin has absorbed it all, dust on refined chalk.

- A cupful of strong coffee will remove the odor of onions from the breath.

A WOMAN'S WORK IS NEVER DONE

Our grandparents worked hard on daily chores and were always looking for short cuts. They seemed to experiment with many chemicals to make their jobs easier. Ammonia was a staple in every home. Some of the cleaning tips are still useful today though I don't think the liberal use of ammonia is wise.

HOUSEHOLD CLEANING TIPS

- 1880's solution for cleaning glass bottles– Crush egg-shells into small bits, or a few carpet tacks, or a small quantity of gunshot, put into the bottle; then fill one-half of strong soapsuds; shake thoroughly, then rinse in clear water. Will look like new.

- 1880's solution - Removing stain from silver caused by eggs- Apply salt with a dry soft cloth.

- 1880's solution - Cleaning glass and mirrors- A soft cloth wet in alcohol is excellent to wipe off plate glass and mirrors, and prevents their becoming frosty in winter.

- 1880's solution - To Brighten Gilt frames- Take sufficient flour of sulphur to give a golden tinge to about one and one-half pints of water, and in this boil four or five bruised onions, or garlic, which will answer the same purpose. Strain off the liquid, and with it, when cold, wash with a soft brush any gilding which requires restoring, and when dry, it will come out as bright as new work.

- 1908 Tip to polish wood floors - Take a strong boiled coffee and strain it twice through a fine strainer, then to three cups of the coffee add one-half cup of common sweet oil and beat well. Put it in a bottle and shake well each time before using. Apply the polish with a soft cloth and then polish with a dry cloth. The coffee drives the oil into the wood, and you will be surprised at the polish you will have on the floors. You only have to put it on once in two weeks.

Now and then just wipe up the floors with a dry mop when they need it, and they look like mirrors.

- To whiten laces, wash them in sour milk.

- A button sewed to the corner of the dish cloth comes in handy to scrape sticky particles from the dishes.

- A small paint brush kept in the kitchen in a handy place will help you keep the crumbs from your toaster.

- Stained Brass - Whiting wet with aqua ammonia, will cleanse brass from stains, and is excellent for polishing faucets and door-knobs of brass or silver. "Sapolio" is still better.

- A good way to clean Mica in a stove that has become blackened with smoke, is to take it out, and thoroughly wash it with vinegar. If the black does not come off at once, let it soak a little.

- Eye glasses can be cleaned with a mixture of half water and half household ammonia. Two drops on a clean cloth will be sufficient to make them shine.

- Fruit stains may be removed from hands by rubbing a tomato over the stains.

- Chewing gum may be removed from clothing by rubbing with the white of an egg.

- Perspiration stains may be removed by dampening the stain with water and sprinkling a little borax upon it. Roll lightly for fifteen minutes, then rinse in cool water.

- To clean white sweaters and other woolen goods without washing - rub thoroughly into material a mixture of 1/3 salt and 2/3 corn meal. Lay aside over night, brush and hang in shade.

- To wipe walls easily and free them from dust, etc., wrap broom in clean flannel cloth.

- Oil paintings may be cleaned by washing very carefully with warm water and milk. Allow to dry without rinsing.

- Piano keys may be cleaned by using a piece of muslin dipped into alcohol. For very yellow keys, use cologne water.

- Clean straw hats by washing with soap and water, then with oxalic acid.

- Silks may be cleaned with potato juice. Get two large potatoes and grate them into a pint of water, this proportion applying to the amount you desire to use. Let the potato starch settle to the bottom, then pour out the clear liquid and bottle it. Lay silk upon a board, apply the potato juice with a sponge until silk is clean. Rinse in cold water

DYING CLOTHES

We take colors in our clothes for granted today but our ancestors had to dye their clothes for colors.

Here are a few of their dye recipes for silk from an old 1880's cookbook.

DYEING OR COLORING – GENERAL REMARKS

Everything should be clean. The goods should be scoured in soap and the soap rinsed out. They are often steeped in soap lye over night. Dip them into water before putting into preparations, to prevent spotting. Soft water should be used sufficient to cover the goods well; this is always understood where quantity is not mentioned. When goods are dyed, air them; then rinse well, and hang up to dry. Do not wring silk or merino dresses when scouring or dyeing them. If cotton goods are to be dyed a light color, they should first be bleached.

SILK DYING

- BLACK - Make a weak lye as for black or woolens; work goods in bichromate of potash a little below boiling heat, then dip in the logwood in the same way; if colored in blue vitriol dye, use about the same heat.

- ORANGE – For one pound goods, annotto one pound, soda one pound; repeat as desired.

- GREEN -VERY HANDSOME -For one pound goods, yellow oak bark eight ounces; boil one-half hour; turn off the liquor from bark and add alum six ounces; let it stand until cold; while making this, color goods in blue dye-tub a light blue, dry and wash, dip in alum and bark dye. It it does not take well, warm the dye a little.

- LIGHT BLUE – For cold water one gallon, dissolve alum one-half tablespoonful, in hot water one teacupful, and add to it; then add chemic, one teaspoonful at a time to obtain the desired color – the more chemic the darker the color.

- PURPLE-For one pound goods. First obtain a light blue, by dipping in home-made dye-tub; then dry; dip in alum four ounces, with water to cover, when little warm. If color in not full enough add chemic.

- YELLOW- For one pound goods, alum three ounces, sugar of lead three-fourths ounce; immerse goods in solution over night, take out, drain, and make a new lye with fustic one pound; dip until the required color is obtained.

- CRIMSON-For one pound goods, alum three ounces; dip at hand heat one hour; take out and drain while making new dye by boiling ten minutes, chochineal three ounces, bruised nutgalls two ounces and cream of tartar one-fourth ounce, in one pail of water; when little cool, begin to dip, raising heat to boil; dip one hour; wash and dry.

- SKY BLUE on SILK or COTTON – VERY BEAUTIFUL- Give goods as much color from a solution of blue vitriol two ounces, to water one gallon, as it will take up in dipping fifteen minutes; then run it through lime water . This will make a beautiful and durable sky blue.

- BROWN on SILK or COTTON – VERY BEAUTIFUL – After obtaining a blue color as above, run goods through a solution of prussiate of potash one ounce, to water one gallon.

DYING WOOL

- CHROME BLACK – BEST IN USE: For five pounds of goods, blue vitriol six ounces; boil a few minutes, then dip the goods three-fourths of an hour, airing often; take out the goods, make a dye with three pounds of logwood, boil one-half hour; dip three-fourths of an hour, air goods, and dip three-fourths of an hour more. Wash in strong suds. This will not fade by exposure to sun.

- WINE COLOR: For five pounds of goods, camwood two pounds; boil fifteen minutes and dip the goods one-half hour; boil again and dip one-half hour; then darken with blue vitriol one and one-half ounces; if not dark enough, add copperas one-half ounce.

- SCARLET-VERY FINE: For one pound of goods, cream of tartar one-half ounce, cochineal, well pulverized, one-half ounce, muriate of tin two and one-half ounces; boil up the dye and enter the goods; work them briskly for ten or fifteen minutes, then boil one and one-half hours, stirring goods slowly while boiling. Wash in clear water and dry in the shade.

- PINK: For three pounds of goods, alum three ounces; boil

and dip the goods one hour, then add to the dye, cream of tartar four ounces, chochineal, well pulverized, one ounce; boil well and dip the goods while boiling until the color suits.

SIMPLE HOME REPAIRS FROM THE PAST

- Stop floors from squeaky by sprinkling talcum powder over them. Sweep the powder into the cracks between the boards

- By dipping a new broom in hot salt water before using, will toughen the bristles and make it last much longer.

- Remove a stripped screw out of its hole by holding a putty knife under the screw head while you turn the screw driver.

- Patch small holes in screens by dabbing them with clear nail polish.

- STICKING DRAWER AND WINDOWS - Rub sticking drawers and windows with candles, paraffin, or soap for easier opening.

- CLEANING FIREPLACES - Dirty brick or stone fireplaces can be cleaned with: 1 cup dishwasher detergent and 1 quart of water, chlorine bleach, soap pads - Rinse well and allow to air dry.

- REMOVING SCRATCHES FROM WOOD FURNITURE - Rub Camphor oil into scratches to fill light or dark wood. The darker the wood, the more you need. Rub the meat of walnuts into walnut wood. Fill cherry or mahogany wood by applying iodine with a cotton swab or toothpick

- A suitable crack filler for floors can be made from a paste of salt, boiling water, and alum. Pour the paste into the cracks and it will be set like cement.

- A red-hot iron will soften old putty so that it can be easily removed.

- CREAKING OF BEDSTEADS - If a bedstead creaks at each movement of the sleeper, remove the slats and wrap the ends of each in old newspapers.

PAINTING TIPS

- Put a strong rubber band lengthwise around your paint can when painting so that the band will make a "bridge" across the top. Use the band to wipe excess paint off the brush as you work. Sides and top of can will stay clean.

- Avoid scraping paint from windows - Cut strips of newspaper the length and width of the window pane and dip in water and they will stick on easily. Then as soon as you are through painting, pull the paper off and you don't have to do any scraping.

- When painting steps, paint every other step, let dry, then paint the remaining ones. Painted in this way the stairs may be walked on without injuring the paint.

- Turn your paint can upside down for 24 hours before using. Paint will mix better.

- Spray hot vinegar on old paint on windowpanes. This softens the paint and makes it easy to scrape off.

- REMOVING PAINT FROM WINDOW PANES -Remove paint splatters on window panes with hot vinegar.

- If there is but a small amount of paint left in a can to be stored, pour paraffin over it before putting it away and it will not dry out but can be used to the last bit.

- A paper plate fastened to the bottom of your paint can with glue, cement or paint: catches the drops and provides a handy place to lay the brush.

- When varnishing floors or linoleum in cold weather; put varnish in a small dish, then place in a larger dish containing hot water. Varnish spreads more uniformly and goes much farther that way.

- If one will rub vaseline on hands before starting a painting job, the paint will wash off easily.

- When painting and you have to keep the house shut up; put 1 ounce of vanilla to half gallon of paint. Will be no scent.

- Oil Painting - When painting the ceiling, take half of an old rubber ball and cut a hole in the bottom. Put the handle of the brush into it. The paint will not run down the handle.

- A pail of water set in a freshly painted room will remover the odor.

- To prevent scum forming over left-over paint in can, pout a little linseed oil over paint before sealing or put 1 tablespoon of paint in groove before forcing the lid on can.

- Hard paint brushes may be softened by soaking in water in which a little lye has been added.

HOUSEHOLD TIPS FROM THE PAST

- Brighten yellowed nylon or linen by adding 1 /4 cup baking soda to your wash along with the detergent.

- Remove a dab of tar or sticky substance from carpet by rubbing in vegetable oil, then blotting it up. Then was with mild soap and water.

- Remove bloodstain from carpet by sprinkling salt over the spot, then cold water. Blot the area with a wet sponge, then paper towels until dry.

- Ribbon or lace will dry flat after washing and need no ironing if it is smoothed around a clean bottle to dry.

- When ironing shirt collars, place a bath towel under collar and iron on wrong side.

- Natural fire extinguishers - Throw baking soda on blaze. It smothers the fire by generating carbonic acid gas which envelops the flames and extinguishes the fire.

- A bent pipe cleaner is useful in getting dirt out of the corner of a camera. Bend half an inch over sharply to get a covered end.

- When lining dresser drawers or cupboard shelves, cut 3 layers of paper. Place all at once. When the top one is soiled, slip off the top one and there's a clean one ready.

- To remove dents in a wooden bowl or bread board, cover the dent with a damp cloth and steam with an iron.

- Candles last longer if placed in refrigerator for a few days before using. They hold their shape better and burn slowly after this treatment.

- The blade of a knife passed through a flame will slice fresh bread more smoothly and easily than a cold blade.

- Put a zipper on ironing board cover to keep it in place and remove easier.

- To make light switches visible at night, paint with luminous paint.

- If the inside of your linen closet is painted a deep blue, there will be no danger of your linens turning yellow. It will eliminate the annoyance of having to wrap those you do not use too often in blue paper.

REMOVING ODORS

- A little lime in a small pan placed in a closet or corner which is damp and musty will keep it dry and odorless. Renew lime every two or three weeks.

- Kitchen odors can be removed by placing an orange peel upon the top of stove while in use.

- A piece of bread on top of pan while cooking cauliflower or cabbage will keep it odorless.

- A small amount of charcoal in a dish kept in the refrigerator will absorb unpleasant odors. Renew every two or three weeks.

- A few drops of oil of wintergreen in corner of refrigerator will accomplish the same result.

- Place pieces of white bread in refrigerator to absorb odors.

- Foods that have boiled over in stove or in oven will not smoke or emit odors if covered with salt.

- To prevent the odor of boiling ham or cabbage, throw red pepper pods or a a few bits of charcoal into the pan they are cooking in.

- Odors may be removed from jars and bottles by filling half full of coll water with one tablespoon dry mustard. Let set for half hour, then rinse in clear water.

- If you're planning to re-use a pickle jar, or any jar which has stored a pungent food, fill the jar with a mixture of water and dry mustard. Let it stand a few hours and all the odors will be removed.

FLOWERS & GARDENING

- Cut flowers keep longer if placed in leftover tea, weakened with water. This is also good for house plants.

- Short-stemmed flowers can be kept fresh by placing them in a bowl or vase of sand that is well moistened.

- A tablespoon of household bleach added to the water in a vase of zinnias will keep the stems from rotting and you will have fresh flowers longer.

- Put a teaspoon of sugar in vase of marigolds and it will help to eliminate the odor.

- Cut flowers will keep longer and stay fresher if an aspirin is put in the water.

- To make geraniums bloom, use bloody chicken water.

- Insert a few rusty nails in the soil around your African violets. The blossoms will be larger, more profuse and will have a brighter color. Keep in north window and water from the bottom

- Did you know that if you pour 2 tablespoons of castor oil around the roots of your Christmas cactus in October it will bloom in December?

- A few drops of castor oil dripped on the dirt in your plant can about every six weeks makes your plants greener and they will blossom better.

- To keep plants watered when leaving for a few days, place on top of pot a sponge soaked with water.

- Eggshells make plants grow. Save them, crush, put in large jar filled with water. Use this water on plants.

- House plants with thick leaves, such as rubber plants, will be benefited greatly by dropping a teaspoon of sweet oil around their roots once a month. It will make the leaves lovely and glossy.

- One of the best fertilizers for potted plants is chimney soot, provided it is free from salt.

- To make a fern healthy and grow fast, put a piece of fresh meat in the pot every few weeks; must not be salty.

- To nourish a fern put 2 raw oysters under the soil near the roots and the plant will grow like magic.

- To water tiny seedlings, dip a wisk broom in water, then sprinkle lightly.

- Use the ribs of an old umbrella for your Morning-glories to climb on.

- Use ice cubes to water indoor plants. They will melt slowly and will not spill over.

- To keep flowers fresh for cemetery. Mix wet sand in container and place flowers in it. Will keep them fresh for a week.

- Rose bush slips will take root if you stick the stem in a white potato.

- Water plants once every two weeks with 5 drops of ammonia and 1 teaspoon soda in 1 quart water.

- Mix coffee grounds with dirt to set geraniums in. Increases both growth and bloom.

- Turn fruit jars over earliest planted vegetables. They will come up quicker.

- Plant sunflowers with your pole beans. Saves time spent in cutting poles and also protects beans from frost.

- Plant radish and cucumber seeds together to keep bugs off cucumbers.

- Gather flowers early in the morning when the plants are less stressed by heat.

- Cut herbs while the dew is still on them on the morning of what will be a hot day. Herbs that have not flowered will be richest in oils.

- Weed your garden after a rainstorm when the roots are easier to pull out.

- Weed your window boxes with a long-handled two-tined cooking fork.

- Tie paper sacks over bunches of grapes and they will keep on the vines many weeks longer.
- To paint flower pots easily, knot a rope and run it through the hole in the pot, leaving the knot inside, then suspend the pot upside down and paint. Allow the paint to dry in this manner.

- Ice water should never be used on house plants as it checks their growth. Add enough hot water to the cold to make it tepid before putting on the plants.

- To keep flowers from dying when leaving home for several days, fold a newspaper and put under each pot in a tub of water.

- Place about two inches in the tub. Soil will stay moist and plant will be all right.

- Gloxinia or African Violet leaves may be rooted by putting the stem through an empty spool and floating in a glass of water.

- Do not over-water cactus plants. Moderate moisture is needed. If over-watered a Christmas cactus will drop its buds.

- A home made frog for flowers: Take paraffin, melt and mold into desired size and shape. Make holes while still warm. The paraffin will float and lets stems of flowers reach into the water. In changing water; frogs may be removed without disarranging.

- When sending flowers by mail, especially roses, dip about two inches of the stems in melted paraffin wax. This holds the moisture in the stems.

- Pansies can be neatly arranged in a shallow dish by inserting the stems through mosquito netting stretched over an embroidery hoop.

SEWING TIPS FROM THE PAST

- To sharpen scissors in an emergency, cut aluminum foil several times.

- Talcum Powder can be used for hem markers.

- Slivers of soap can be used for marking hems on washable fabrics.

- Silk thread is the best type to use in sewing wool.

- After lowering the hem on a wool garment, sponge the old hemline with vinegar before pressing to remove the telltale crease.

- When mending a large hole in a sweater, reinforce the hole with net. This forms a good foundation for darning, and will prevent puckering.

COST SAVING TIPS

- Save old match boxes and use them for molds when making homemade soap. Simply tear away the box portion when ready to use.

- Do not throw away that old popcorn. It you can't make it pop, put it in a jar, add 1 tablespoon water and let stand a week or two. It will pop.

EAT, DRINK AND BE MERRY

In the childhood memories of every good cook, there's a large kitchen, a warm stove, a simmering pot and a grandmother. Our grandparents put a lot of 'love' into their cooking.

COOKING TIPS

- Lumpy gravy can be avoided by adding a little salt to the flour before adding the water and stirring with a fork.

- In frying with lard, keep lard from spattering by sprinkling a little salt in it. Articles will not absorb too much lard if they are fried in lard to which a teaspoonful of vinegar has been added.

- Marshmallows may be cut without sticking to the knife if knife is dipped into very hot water first.

- Eggs should be cooked slowly at moderate heat. Fast cooking will toughen the whites of the eggs.

- Carrots peeled under warm water will not leave stain on hands.

- Brown sugar placed in bread box will help keep bread fresh.

- Cook spinach in open top pan and the color will be retained.

- Lemon juice or vinegar rubbed over steak before cooking will make meat more tender

PRESERVING FOOD

- For potatoes, carrots and beets; sink a bottomless box or barrel in the earth, cover bottom with dry hay or straw and lay roots on top. Or dig a pit and line it with stones. But be sure there is good drainage. For turnips, rutabagas, and winter radishes, if you have a dry whitewashed cellar, store in bins on the cellar floor. Fill some of the bins with will dried sand and bury root vegetables in the sand, keeping out some to blanch for salad. For sand burial parsnips, Jerusalem artichokes, kohlrabi, salsify, winter radishes, horseradish, carrots, and celeriac are suitable.

- Place the egg in a pan of water....If fresh, it will lie on its side, if a few days old, it will tilt upwards. If stale, it will stand on end..If very old, it will float.

OLD MEASUREMENTS

- A handful of dry ingredients equals about 1/4 cup

- A clenched fist held up-right approximates the volume of 1 cup liquid measure

- A pinch is about 1/8 teaspoon.

- Butter the size of an egg means about 4 tablespoons or 1/4 cup

- A teacupful means about 1/2 cup.

EQUIVALENT OVEN TEMPERATURE FROM OLD RECIPES

- A low oven is 250 degrees F.

- A slow oven is 300 degrees F.

- A moderate oven is 350 degrees F.

- A hot oven is 400 degrees F.

- A very hot oven is 450 degrees F.

- Broil is 550 degrees F.

UNUSUAL MEASURES AND WEIGHTS FROM 1880s

- 4 teaspoonfuls equal 1 tablespoonful liquid

- 2 Tablespoonfuls equal 1 wine-glass, or half a gill

- 2 Wine-glasses equal one gill or half a cup

- 2 Gills equal 1 coffeecupful, or 16 tablespoonfuls

- 3 Coffecupfuls equal 1 pint

- An ordinary tumblerfull equal 1 coffeecupfull, or half a pint

- About 25 drops of any thin liquid will fill a common sized teaspoon.

MISCELLANEOUS COOKING TIPS

- To make carrots curl, slice very thin length wise. Drop in ice and water, the curl is natural and permanent.

- Onions will not make the eyes water if scalding water is poured over them before they are peeled.

- Rub scissors with butter to cut up marshmallows

- When peeling onions, put a slice of bread in your mouth.

- When making a lemon pie, instead of grating the lemon rind, boil the rind in the water before adding the sugar. The flavor is just as good and it saves time.

- To make a roast, chicken or turkey tender, place 2 eight penny new nails in the roaster, as you put on the roast. It makes them cook twice as quick. Always use new nails each time.

- For extra flavor in chocolate cakes, dust your greased cake pan with sifted cocoa instead of flour.

- Keep leftover cake moist by attaching pieces of bread with toothpicks to exposed edges of the cake.

- Butter the rim of the pan in which you cook rice or pasta to prevent the water from boiling over.

- For a clear, not opaque sauces, use cornstarch to thicken them.

- To freshen slightly wilted lettuce, add a little lemon juice to a bowl of cold water. Put the lettuce in it for about an hour.

- When cracking a large quantity of nuts for your holiday recipes, put them in a pillowcase and tap lightly with a hammer until they're all cracked.

- Put your oranges in a hot oven for a couple of minutes before you peel them. They'll peel much easier, and without the white fibers that usually stick to the fruit.

- Brush the bottom crust of meat pie, with the white of an egg to prevent the gravy soaking in.

- Shortly before taking cup cakes from the oven, place a marshmallow on each for the frosting.

- To keep cookies fresh and crisp in the jar, place a crumpled tissue paper in the bottom.

- Put cream or milk on top of two-crust pies for a nice brown pie.

- Keeping cake Fresh: To keep a loaf or layer cake fresh after it has been cut, wrap a large slice of fresh bread in with it before putting it away. The bread will dry out but the cake will remain moist.

- To see whether old yeast is still good, put it in warm water with a teaspoon of sugar and stir. If it begins to foam in 10 minutes, you can use it with your flour right away.

- For even consistency, when making pie crust. Add water with clothes sprinkler.

- Add a little salt to jello salads and desserts. It improves the flavor. Add a little sugar to vegetables while cooking. It improves the flavor. Add a banana to rhubarb pie, the flavor will resemble pineapple.

- Put cream or milk on top of two-crust pies for a nice brown pie.

- Store cake in vegetable or fruit drawer of refrigerator and it will stay fresh.

- When bread is baking, a small dish of water in the oven will help to keep the crust from getting hard.

- An apple cut in half and placed in the cake box will keep the cake fresh several days longer.

- When icing a cake, the icing will not run off if a little flour is dusted on the surface of the cake.

- To keep crisp cookies crisp, and soft cookies soft, place only one kind in a cookie jar.

- If you want to make a pecan pie, and haven't any nuts, substitute crushed cornflakes. They will rise to the top the same as nuts and give a delicious flavor and crunchy surface.

- Cooked onions will stay perfectly whole if you poke a hole through the center of each one with a metal skewer before cooking.

- Chewing gum while peeling onions helps to prevent tears.

- Soak potatoes in salt water for 20 minutes before baking them and they will bake more rapidly.

- Never salt turnips while they're cooking. It exacts their sweetness and puts them in the cowfeed class.

- Add a teaspoon of sugar to each quart of water when boiling corn-on-the-cob. This improves the flavor.

- Sweet potatoes will not turn dark if put in salted water immediately after peeling, using 5 teaspoons salt to 1 quart of water.

- Fresh tomatoes will keep longer if placed with stems down.

- To freshen vegetables add a little vinegar to the water when washing them.

- To remove the skins from carrots easily, drop into boiling water and let stand for a few minutes.

- Candying apples - fried apples will candy nicely if a little bit of salt is added to the pan

- Salt sprinkled on grapefruit will bring out the natural flavor and reduce any bitter taste

- Sprinkle lemon juice on sliced bananas or sliced apples to keep them fresh

- Add a teaspoon of sugar to each quart of water when boiling corn-on-the-cob. This improves the flavor.

- The best way to get corn silks off the cob is with a stiff vegetable brush.

- To pep up buttered corn. Saute a bit of green pepper in

butter before adding corn.

- For people who say they can't eat onions – soak the onions in milk before using them.

- Slice and peel pounds of onions without a tear. Slice them first with the heavy blade of a chef's knife, then just slip off the skin.

- Cooked onions will stay perfectly whole if you poke a hole through the center of each one with a metal skewer before cooking.

- If you spread the meringue on the pie so that it touches the crust on each side and bake in a moderate oven, it should not shrink.

- Use 2 tablespoons of minute tapioca to thicken your pies instead of flour.

- When sweetening rhubarb pie, substitute 2 tablespoons of red colored sugar for the regular sugar. The result is a beautifully colored and appetizing pie.

- When making Blueberry, Elderberry or any flat berry pie instead of adding lemon juice or vinegar try 1 teaspoon of salt to a small pie and 1 ½ teaspoons to a large pie. Stir well and see how this will bring out the flavor of the berry.

- Do you throw out a lot of old coffee in your home? Don't waste the beverage; sweeten it and add some plain gelatin, then mold and you have a perfect and simple dessert, served with cream, of course.

- While your custard is still hot, and before you put it in the refrigerator to chill, cover it with waxed paper or a bowl cover. This will keep a scum from forming on the top.

- Use 2 tablespoons of minute tapioca to thicken your pies

instead of flour.

- Too much sugar, too intense heat or too long cooking will cause custard to be watery.

- It takes 6 eggs to a quart of milk to make a perfect baked custard

- Put layer of marshmallows in bottom of pumpkin pie, then filling, marshmallows will come to top and make nice topping.

- Half a small jar of jam or jelly folded in a cup of cream whipped stiff will turn out a nice topping for puddings.

- In making rhubarb, cherry or any berry pie that is very juicy, try beating an egg light, and mixing in the sugar required by the fruit; add a little flour, mix thoroughly and then bake as usual. In this way, excess of juice will be in the pie and not in the bottom of the oven.

- In making fruit pies, put sugar in between two layers of fruit as sugar next to top crust toughens it.

- To avoid heating up the kitchen to brown meringue, heat a heavy iron skillet and turn upside down over meringue until golden brown.

- When making juicy pies, cut the lower crust one half inch larger than the top. Fold it over like a hem; the juice will not leak out readily.

- When making raisin pie, a little lemon juice or vinegar added will improve the flavor.

- Add fresh grated coconut to vanilla ice cream and serve with rich chocolate sauce. This will not be found in any reducing diet. But it tastes like more.

- Half a small jar of jam or jelly folded in a cup of cream whipped stiff will turn out a nice topping for puddings.

- When making egg custard pies, always heat the milk to the boiling point before mixing with the eggs. It this rule is followed, the under-crust will be crisp.

- When making apple pies, if you put a layer of apples in your crust then your sugar, cinnamon and lemon juice or whatever you use, then apples on top of the sugar again, your pie will not run over in the oven.

- A delicious whipped cream substitute is easily made by adding a sliced banana to the whites of one beaten egg and beating until stiff. The banana will completely dissolve.

- You should not pile together left over potatoes, as they sour quickly.

- If you want to make a pecan pie and haven't any nuts, substitute crushed cornflakes. They will rise to the top the same as nuts and give a delicious flavor and crunchy surface.

- To cut meringue pies easily, sift a little granulated sugar over the meringue just before it is browned in the oven. This makes a pretty crust and makes the pie easy to cut.

- A good quick frosting is made by boiling a small potato, mashing it, and adding powdered sugar and vanilla.

- Use milk instead of water in making pie crust. It makes it more tender and browns nicely.

- To keep crisp cookies crisp, and soft cookies soft, place only one kind in a cookie jar.

- Use milk instead of water in making pie crust. It makes it more tender and browns nicely.

- Any cake will be greatly improved if a teaspoon of lemon juice is added to the butter and sugar. This makes a cake very light and shorter. Fresh mild makes cakes close grained and more solid.

- For a nice decoration on white frosting, shave colored gumdrops very thin and stick on. They will curl like little roses.

- Too much liquid will make a cake that falls easily.

- When baking bread, a small dish of water in the oven will help keep the crust from getting too hard or brown.

- The eyes will not water when peeling onions if real hot water is poured over onions.

- Oranges, apples, beets, peaches and tomatoes will peel much easier if scalded first.

- A tablespoon of vinegar added to beets in cooking will help keep the color and also to cook faster.

- Lemon or orange juice sprinkled on sliced bananas will keep them from turning dark.

- Cook spinach in open top pan and the color will be retained.

- Cookies and cake which have become dry or stale can be made fresh again by putting in box with bread - or by dipping in milk and rebaking.

- Lemon juice or vinegar rubbed over steak before cooking will make meat more tender

- Use milk rather than water in your flour dough results in a finer texture.

- To keep boiled syrup from crystallizing, add a pinch of

baking soda

- When icing a cake, the icing will not run off it a little flour is dusted on the surface of the cake.

- Bake gingerbread in cup cake pans. When cold, cut out center, fill with cream cheese and quince jelly. Serve with coffee.

- For flakier pie crusts add a teaspoon of vinegar to the cold water in preparing your pie dough.

- Sugar in fried cakes, fritters,etc., should always be added to the milk—this prevents the cakes from absorbing the fat in the frying.

- Refrigerate your heavy cream before beating and it will whip up much faster. It also helps if the bowl and beaters are cold as well.

- Wine that has soured may be used in place of vinegar, especially in meat marinades.

- When your celery goes limp, just submerge it in ice water along with a thin slice of Irish potato and it will perk right up.

- Let chocolate cake cool 5 minutes before taking it from the pan. Turn an angel food or sponge cake upside down as soon as it is removed from the oven. Let it hang for an hour. Then take from the pan.

- One teaspoon of vanilla in cranberries is good.

- In colonial days, preserving meat for the winter or for use during travel was a major concern before canning and usually kept for years, not months. Food was preserved by drying or parching in several ways. Meats were cut thin and usually salted, then placed over a slow fire for jerky on in the sun or wind. Large chunks of meat were usually impregnated in dry salt or a brine solution and then slowly smoked and dried. Smoking and drying meat required outdoor temperatures below forty degrees to preserve the meat during the extensive early stages, so it was only done late in the year.

HINTS FOR CANNING

- When making jelly and jam, hang a piece of string over the edges of the glass before pouring in the paraffin. This makes it easier to remove paraffin when opened for table use.

- A vegetable brush is just the thing to remove scum from jelly or soup.

- To clean can lids, put lids in a pan. Cover with sweet milk, let stand till clabbered, then take out and wash. They are like new.

- A little lime kept on shelves where jellies or preserves are stored, will usually prevent formation of mold.

- Jam or jelly that is hard or sugary will be like new if you leave it in a warm oven until the sugar softens.

- Prevent a jar of jam or jelly from spoiling, place a cloth soaked in vinegar over the jar before you put the lid on.

- A small amount of butter added to the fruit when cooking eliminates the usual foam which forms on the top.

- Juice left over form canned fruit is excellent when thickened and served over plain cake and cottage pudding.

RECIPES FROM THE PAST

MARMALADE PUDDING (1867)

Take about a half a teacupful of milk, one tablespoonful of fine flour, and about two ounces of white sugar; put it on the fire, and stir it till it boils; then add the yolks of four eggs, and one small pot of marmalade, reserving most of the chips to line the mould; mix all well together, then beat up the whites of five eggs, and stir them lightly in. Butter a mould, and line it completely with orange chips; put in the pudding, and steam it for half an hour with fire under and over.

BLUEBERRY PICKLES (1880's)

For blueberry pickles, old jars which have lost their covers, or whose edges have been broken so that the covers will not fit tightly, serve an excellent purpose, as these pickles must not be kept air-tight.

Pick over your berries, using only sound ones; fill your jars or wide-mouthed bottles to within an inch of the top, then pour in molasses enough to settle down into all the spaces; this cannot be done in a moment, as molasses does not run very freely. Only lazy people will feel obliged to stand by and watch the progress. As it settles, pour in more until the berries are covered. Then tie over the top a piece of cotton cloth to keep the flies and other insects out and set away in the preserve closet. Cheap molasses is good enough, and your pickles will soon be "sharp." Wild grapes may be pickled in the same manner

PEAR PICKLE (1880's)

Select small, sound ones, remove the blossom end, stick them with a fork, allow to each quart of pears one pint of cider vinegar and one cup of sugar, put in a teaspoonful allspice, cinnamon and cloves to boil with the vinegar; then add the pears and boil, and seal in jars.

SPICED PLUMS (1880's)

Seven pounds of plums, one pint of cider vinegar, four pounds of sugar, two tablespoonfuls of broken cinnamon bark, half as much of whole cloves and the same of broken nutmeg; place these in a muslin bag and simmer them in a little vinegar and water for half an hour; then add it all to the vinegar and sugar, and bring to a boil; add the plums and boil carefully until they are cooked tender. Before cooking the plums they should be pierced with a darning needle several times; this will prevent the skins bursting while cooking.

PORK & BEANS (baked) (1880's)

Take two quarts of white beans, pick them over the night before, put to soak in cold water; in the morning put them in fresh water and let them scald, then turn off the water and put on more, hot; put to cook with them a piece of salt pork, gashed, as much as would make five or six slices; boil slowly till soft (not mashed), then add a tablespoonful of molasses, half a teaspoonful of soda, stir in well, put in deep pan, and bake one hour and a half. If you do not like to use pork, salt the beans when boiling, and add a lump of butter when preparing them for the oven.

OX TAIL SOUP (1880's)

Two ox-tails, two slices of ham, one ounce of butter, two carrots, two turnips, three onions, one leek, one head of celery, one bunch of savory herbs, pepper, a tablespoonful of salt, two tablespoonfuls of catsup, one-half glass of port wine, three quarters of water.

Cut up the tails, separating them at the joints; wash them, and put them in a stewpan with the butter. Cut the vegetables in slices and add them with the herbs. Put in one-half pint of water, and stir it over a quick fire till the juices are drawn. Fill up the stewpan with water, and when boiling, add the salt. Skim well, and simmer very gently for four hours, or until the tails are tender. Take them out, skim and strain the soup, thicken with flour, and flavor with the catsup and port wine. Put back the tails, simmer for five minutes and serve.

TIMBALE OF MACARONI

Break in very short lengths small macaroni (vermicelli, spaghetti, tagliarini). Let it be rather overdone; dress it with butter and grated cheese, then work into it one or two eggs, according to quantity, Butter and bread crumb a plain mold, and when the macaroni is nearly cold fill the mold with it, pressing it well down and leaving a hollow in the centre, into which place a well-flavored mince of meat, poultry or game; then fill up the mold with more macaroni, pressed well down. Bake in a moderately heated oven, turn out and serve.

BATTALIA PIE (1772)

Take four small chickens, and squab pigeons, four sucking rabbits, cut them in pieces, and season them with savory spice, lay them in the pie, with four sweetbreads slice, as many sheeps tongues and shivered palates, two pair of lambs stones, twenty or thirty cockscombs, with savoury balls and oysters; lay on butter, and close the pie with a lear.

QUEENS CAKE (1772)

Take a pound of sugar, and beat it fine, pour in yolks and two whites of eggs, half a pound of butter, a little rose water, six spoonfuls of warm cream, a pound of currants, and as much flour as will make it up; stir them well together, and put them into your patty pans, being well buttered; bake them in an oven; almost as hot as for manchet for half an hour; then take them out and glaze them, and let them stand but a little after the glazing is on, to rise.

Scuppernongs are high in Vitamin C and contain potassium, Vitamin B, trace minerals, are naturally low in sodium and free of fat and cholesterol...Here is a recipe for Scuppernong juice. Keep it and when those scuppernongs ripen...you will be prepared.

SCUPPERNONG JUICE

1. Crush thoroughly 3 pounds (about 9 cups or 4 pints) fully ripe scuppernongs.
2. Add 1 cup water. Cover and simmer 10 minutes.
3. Strain through jelly bag or cheese cloth.
4. Refrigerate and serve, or use in jelly or pie recipes.

SNOW BIRDS (1900's)

One dozen thoroughly cleaned birds; stuff each with an oyster, put them into a yellow dish, and add two ounces of boiled salt pork and three raw potatoes cut into slices; add a pint of oyster liquor, an ounce of butter; salt and pepper; cover the dish with a crust and bake in moderate oven.

ROAST PIGEONS (1900's)

Pigeons lose their flavor by being kept more than a day after they are killed. They maybe prepared and roasted or broiled the same as chickens; they will require from twenty to thirty minutes' cooking. Make a gravy of the giblets or not, season it with pepper and salt, and add a little flour and butter.

TURKEY HASH (1900's)

Cut the remnants of turkey from a previous dinner into pieces of equal size. Boil the bones in a quart of water, until the quart is reduced to a pint, then take out the bones, and to the liquor in which they were boiled add turkey gravy, if you have any, or white stock, or a small piece of butter with salt and pepper; let the liquor thus prepared boil up once; then put in the pieces of turkey, dredge in a little flour, give it one boil-up, and serve in a hot dish.

CORN SOUP (1900's)

Cut the corn from the cob, and boil the cobs in water for at least an hour, then add the grains, and boil until they are thoroughly done; put one dozen ears of corn to a gallon of water, which will be reduced to three quarts by the time the soup is done; then pour on a pint of new milk, two well-beaten eggs, salt and pepper to your taste; continue the boiling a while longer, and stir in, to season and thicken it a little, a tablespoonful of good butter rubbed up with two tablespoonfuls of flour. Corn soup may also be made nicely with water in which a pair of grown fowls have been boiled or parboiled, instead of having plain water for the foundation.

CHICKEN DRESSED IN TERRAPIN (1900's)

Select young chickens, clean and cut them into pieces; put them into a stew pan with just enough water to cook them. When tender stir into a half of a cup of butter and one beaten egg. Season it with salt and pepper, a teaspoonful of powdered thyme; add two hard-boiled eggs coarsely minced and a small glass of wine. Boil up once and serve with jelly.

CODFISH A LA MODE (1900's)

Pick up a teacupful of salt codfish very fine and freshen—the desiccated is nice to use:two cups mashed potatoes, one pint cream or milk, two well-beaten eggs, half a cup butter, salt and pepper; mix; bake in an earthen baking dish from twenty to twenty-five minutes; serve in the same dish, placed on a small platter, covered with a fine napkin.

OLD-FASHIONED APPLESAUCE (1900's)

Pare and chop a dozen medium-sized apples, put them in a deep pudding-dish; sprinkle over them a heaping coffee-cupful of sugar and one of water. Place them in the oven and bake slowly two hours or more, or until they are a deep red brown; quite as nice as preserves.

GRILLED SALT PORK (1900's)

Take quite thin slices of the thick part of side pork, of a clear white, and thinly streaked with lean; hold one on a toasting fork before a brisk fire to grill; have at hand a dish of cold water, in which immerse it frequently while cooking,to remove the superfluous fat and render it more delicate. Put each slice as cooked in a warm covered pan; when all are done, serve hot.

OLD RECIPE FOR IRISH STEW (1890's)

Time about two hours. Two and a half pounds of chops, eight

potatoes, four turnips, four small onions, nearly a quart of water. Take some chops from loin of mutton, place them in stewpan in alternate layers of sliced potatoes and chops; add turnips and onions cut into pieces, pour in nearly a quart of cold water; cover stewpan closely, let it stew gently till vegetables are ready to mash and the greater part of the gravy is absorbed; then place in a dish; serve it up hot.

SCRAMBLED MUTTON (1890's)

Two cups of chopped cold mutton, two tablespoonfuls of hot water, and a piece of butter as large as an English walnut.
When the meat is hot, break in three eggs, and constantly stir until the eggs begin to stiffen, Season with pepper and salt.

STEAMED POTATOES (1890's)

This mode of cooking potatoes is now much in vogue, particularly where they are wanted on a large scale, it being so very convenient. Pare the potatoes, throw them into cold water as they are peeled, then put them in a steamer.

Place the steamer over a saucepan of boiling water, and steam the potatoes from twenty to forty minutes, according to the size and sort. When the fork goes easily through them,they are done; then take them up, and serve very quickly.

POTATO SNOW (1890's)

Choose some mealy potatoes that will boil exceedingly white; pare them and cook them well, but not so as to be watery; drain them, and mash and season them well. Put in the saucepan in which they were dressed, so as to keep them as hot as possible; then press them through a wire sieve into the dish in which they are to be served; strew a little fine salt upon them previous to sending them to table. French cooks also add a small quantity of pounded loaf sugar while they are being mashed.

SHORT'NIN' BREAD (1900's)

4 cups flour
1 pound butter
1 cup light brown sugar

Combine sugar and flour. Add butter. Place on floured board and pat to thickness of one-half inch. Cut into shapes desired and bake in a moderate oven. (325-350º) for twenty to twenty-five minutes.

MOLASSES PUDDING (1900's)

2 tablespoons of sugar 1 egg
½ cup of molasses 1 pinch salt
1 ½ cup of flour 1 teaspoon baking soda dissolved
½ cu of boiling water in hot water
2 tablespoons of melted butter

Beat the egg and sugar, add the butter, water, soda, and molasses and then beat in the flour and salt. Put in a double boiler and steam for one hour. Serve with your favorite fruit sauce.

PICKLED CHICKEN

Boil four chickens till tender enough for meat to fall from bones; put meat in a stone jar and pour over it three pints of cold, good cider vinegar and a pint and a half of the water in which the chickens were boiled; add spices if preferred, and it will be ready for use in two days. This is a popular Sunday evening dish; it is good for luncheon at any time.

STEAMED CHICKEN

Rub the chicken on the inside with pepper and half a teaspoonful of salt; place in a steamer in a kettle that will keep it as near the water as possible, cover and steam an hour and a half; when done, keep hot while dressing is prepared, then cut up, arrange on the platter, and serve with the dressing over it.

MOCK TURTLE SOUP OF CALF'S HEAD

Scald a well-cleansed calf's head, remove the brain, tie it up in a cloth, and boil an hour, or until the meat will easily slip from the bone; take out, save the broth; cut it in small square pieces, and throw them into cold water; when cool, put it in a stewpan, and cover with some of the broth; let it boil until quite tender, and set aside.

In another stewpan melt some butter, and in it put a quarter of a pound of lean ham, cut small, with fine herbs to taste; also parsley and one onion; add about a pint of the broth, let it simmer for two hours, and then dredge in a small quantity of flour; now add the remainder of the broth, and a quarter bottle of Madeira or sherry; let all stew quietly for ten minutes and rub it through a medium sieve; add the calf's head, season with a very little cayenne pepper, a little salt, the juice of one lemon, and, if desired, a quarter teaspoonful pounded mace and a dessert-spoon sugar.

Having previously prepared force meat ball, add them to the soup, and five minutes after serve hot.

FORCE MEAT BALLS FOR THE ABOVE:

Six tablespoonfuls of turtle meat chopped very fine. Rub to a paste, with the yolk of two hard-boiled eggs, a tablespoonful of butter, and, if convenient, a little oyster liquor. Season with cayenne, mace, half a teaspoonful of white sugar and a pinch of salt. Bind all with a well-beaten egg; shape into small balls; dip in egg, then powdered cracker; fry in butter, and drop into the soup when it is served.

SNOW PANCAKES

There's no place like the old farm to toss up a batch of snow pancakes, because city snow isn't fit to eat.

Make thick pancake batter by using less milk than your usual recipe calls for. Have griddle hot and ready to go. Rush outdoors and gather one cup of newly fallen snow, light and fluffy as angel feathers, for each pint of milk you've used in the batter. Beat the snow rapidly into the batter and bake your pancakes at once before any of the sparkle of the fresh snow has evaporated. These will be wonderfully light and toothsome.
Old snow positively will not do, not because it may be dirty from lying around, but because it's lost its volatile value- which some cooks claim is ammonia, while others say that's not scientifically correct. Anyway, it makes a great pancake.

SNOW WAFFLES

Follow directions for Snow Pancakes after you've made your favorite waffle batter, with less milk than usual, to allow for the snow.

MILK SOUP

1 quart milk 1 inch lemon peel
2 tablespoons flour ½ teaspoon salt
1-inch cinnamon stick ¼ cup sugar
½ egg yolk

Put flour in a cup and work smooth with a little milk, add a little more milk and let stand. Heat remaining milk and seasonings to a boiling point. Pour flour mixture into hot milk through a sieve, stirring constantly. Simmer and stir for 10-15 minutes. Beat egg yolk in a tureen and stir milk soup into them.

BIRD SOUP

1 grouse or partridge (or less desirable 1 celery stalk
portion of several) Herb bouquet (celery sprig,
2 tablespoons butter parsley,bay leaf)
1 onion, sliced salt and pepper
½ cup diced raw ham 1 ½ quarts meat broth

Cut up birds. Slowly fry in butter with onion, ham, and celery until light brown. Add broth and bouquet and slowly simmer for an hour or more. Strain and press all soft ingredients through a sieve. Thicken if desired with a little flour browned in butter. Add 1 -2 tablespoons sherry or home made wine, and serve with croutons. If a whole bird has been used cut the thick meat from the breast; either cook it in the soup or sauté in butter, dice it an add just before serving.
Any small birds or the carcass of a wild duck may be turned into this soup.

APPLE SLUMP

The original recipe for this old-fashioned New England dish calls for a dozen tart juicy apples. Core, pare and quarter them, put in a heavy kettle (iron if possible) over slow heat with a cup of hot water and let cook 5 minutes. Then pour over 2 cups of molasses (not syrup). Make a biscuit dough crust, adding 1 teaspoon sugar, roll out and cover apples. Cover kettle closely and let contents cook 25 minutes without lifting cover.

FRESH FRUIT PUFFS

1 egg 2 teacups flour
1 cup milk 2 teaspoons baking powder
1 tablespoon butter Fruit
¼ teaspoon salt

Mix ingredients to a smooth batter; put buttered cups in steamer, drop in each 1 tablespoon of batter, then one of berries or diced apples or peaches, cover with batter and steam 30 minutes. Serve with sugar and cream.

HOME BUTCHERED PORK

There should be almost no waste to a fattened hog, ears, feet, tail and sausage casings all having their uses- everything but the squeal, as they say down South. The choicest piece for roasting is the whole backbone with its delicate fillets, after the hams and bacon have been cut off. The upper skin of the ears after parboiling, may be loosened up to make pockets for a delicately seasoned bread stuffing; simmer in a little hard cider. The neck likewise is a piece for stuffing after the bone is removed; it should be baked.

Another delicious bit is the shoulder bone with some meat left on; it cooks rather quickly, with peppercorns and herbs; spread the drained meat with butter and eat with mustard and a dish of greens boiled in its pot liquor. Everyone relishes the feet split and boiled tender with herbs, then egged and crumbed and fried, or chilled in their own reduced jelly, or pickled in spiced vinegar. Spareribs have always been baked and eaten with applesauce and baked potatoes, or simmered with herbs and imbedded (sic) in cooked sauerkraut; but they may be stuffed like poultry, two rounding pieces being sewed together to look like a turkey and receive a dressing of equal portions of bread crumbs, dried currants and chopped apples, before baking.

TOAD IN A HOLE

Cut cooked mutton, veal, beef or fowl into sizable cubes and simmer in leftover gravy with a chopped onion, a chopped leek, a pinch of minced parsley, and a little salt and pepper. Place the pieces of meat well apart in the bottom of a meat pie dish, and arrange mashed potato around each piece, piling it up so that the meat peeks out like a toad in a hole. Drop the gravy with a spoon into the holes and brown in the oven.

The Scotch- American injunction handed down with this old standby is, "Don't cook too much or the family will eat too much."

AN APPLE A DAY KEEPS THE DOCTOR AWAY

We have come a long way in understanding how one stays healthy....this is from a book written prior to 1900.

> "Dr. B. I. Kendall writes that "the temperature of the body should be evenly and properly maintained to secure perfect health; and to accomplish this purpose requires great care and caution at times. The human body is, so to speak, the most delicate and intricate piece of machinery that could possibly be conceived of, and to keep this in perfect order requires constant care.
>
> It is a fixed law of nature that every violation thereof shall be punished; and so we find that he who neglects to care for his body by protecting it from sudden changes of weather, or draughts of cold air upon unprotected parts of the body, suffers the penalty by sickness, which may vary according to exposure and the habits of the person, which affect the result materially; for what would be an easy day's work for a man who is accustomed to hard labor, would be sufficient to excite the circulation to such an extent in a person unaccustomed to work, that only slight exposure might cause death of the latter, when over-heated this way; while the same exercise and exposure to the man accustomed to hard labor might not affect him."

HOW PEOPLE GET SICK (from 1875 publication)

- By eating too much and too fast and by swallowing imperfectly masticated food.

- Keeping up a constant excitement, and fretting the mind with borrowed troubles.

- Wearing thin shoes.

- Keeping late hours at night and sleeping too late in the morning.

HOW TO STAY WELL (1880's)

- Don't sleep in a draught.

- Don't go to bed with cold feet.

- Don't stand over hot air registers.

- Don't eat what you do not need just to save it.

- Don't try to get cool too quickly after exercising.

- Don't sleep in a room without ventilation of some kind.

- Don't stuff a cold lest you should be next obliged to starve a fever.

- Don't sit in a damp or chilly room without a fire.

- Don't try to get along without flannel underclothing in winter.

HOW TO STAY WELL (1900's)

- One should be cautious about entering a sick room in a state of perspiration, as the moment you become cool your pores absorb.

- Do not approach contagious diseases with an empty stomach, nor sit between the sick and the fire, because the heat attracts the vapor.

- The flavor of cod-liver oil may be changed to the delightful one of fresh oyster, if the patient will drink a large glass of water poured from a vessel in which nails have been allowed to rust.

- That well-ventilated bedrooms will prevent morning headaches and lassitude.
- The best time to bathe is just before going to bed, as any danger of taking cold is thus avoided; and the complexion is improved by keeping warm for several hours after leaving the bath.

HOW PEOPLE GET SICK (from 1875 publication)

- By exchanging the warm clothing worn in a warm room during the day for light costumes and exposure incident to evening parties.

- By starving the stomach to gratify the vain and foolish passion for dress.

- Employing cheap doctors, and swallowing quack nostrums for every imaginary ill

HOME REMEDIES FOR COMMON AILMENTS (from 1880 cookbook)

- Nervous spasms are usually relieved by a little salt taken into the mouth and allowed to dissolve.

- Sleeplessness, caused by too much blood in the head, may be overcome by applying a cloth wet with cold water to the back of the neck.

- A drink of hot, strong lemonade before going to bed will often break up a cold and cure a sore throat.

- Sufferers from asthma should get a muskrat skin and wear it over their lungs with the fur side next to the body. It will bring certain relief.

EARLY TO BED AND EARLY TO RISE (From the perfect Woman 1903 by K. T. Boland)

Early rising cannot be too strongly insisted upon; nothing is more conducive to health and thus to a long life. A youth is frequently allowed to spend the early part of the morning in bed, breathing the impure atmosphere of the bedroom; when he should be up and inhaling the balmy and health-giving breezes of the morning.

If early rising is commenced in childhood it becomes a habit; and will continue through life. A boy ought on no account to be roused from his sleep; but as soon as he is awake in the morning he should be encouraged to rise.

Dozing—that state between sleeping and waking—is injurious; it enervates both body and mind and is as detrimental to health as dram drinking. But if he rises early he must go to bed betimes; it is a bad practice to keep him up until the family retires to rest. He ought to seek his pillow by nine o'clock and should rise as soon as he awakes in the morning.

DANGERS OF WATER

(from a book published in 1883 Ladies Guide in Health and Disease, on applications of water)

Water, applied in the various modes in which it may be, is one of the most potent of remedies. Wrongly applied, it may be productive of great harm. The following are a few general rules which should always govern its use:

- Never bathe when exhausted or within three hours after eating, unless the bath be confined to a very small portion of the body.

- Never bathe when cooling off after profuse sweating, as reaction will then often be deficient.

- Always wet the head before taking any form of bath, to prevent determination of blood to the head.

- If the bath be a warm one, always conclude it with an application of water which is a few degrees cooler than the bodily temperature.

- Be careful to thoroughly dry the patient after his bath, rubbing vigorously, to prevent chilling.

- The most favorable time for taking a bath is between the hours of ten and twelve in the forenoon.

- The temperature of the room should be at about 85º or 90º F.

- Baths should usually be of a temperature which will be the most agreeable to the patient. Cold baths are seldom required. Too much hot bathing is debilitating.

HERB REMEDIES BLOOD PURIFIER

- Mandrake root one ounce, dandelion root one ounce, burdock root one ounce, yellow duck root one ounce, prickly ash berries two ounces, marsh mallow one ounce, turkey rhubarb half an ounce, gentian one ounce, English camomile (sic) flowers one ounce, red clover tops two ounces.

- Wash the herbs and roots; put them into an earthen vessel, pour over two quarts of water that has been boiled and cooled; let it stand over night and soak; in the morning set it on the back of the stove, and steep it five hours; it must not boil, but be nearly ready to boil. Strain it through a cloth, and add half a pint of good gin. Keep it in a cool place. Half a wine-glass taken as a dose twice a day.

67

- This is better than all the paten blood medicines that are in the market-a superior blood purifier, and will cure almost any malignant sore, by taking according to direction, and washing the sore with a strong tea of red raspberry leaves steeped, first washing the sore with castile soap, then drying with a soft cloth, and washing it with the strong tea of red raspberry leaves.

POULTICES (1900's)

- BREAD AND MILK POULTICE – Put a tablespoonful of the crumbs of stale bread into a gill of milk, and give the whole one boil up. Or, take stale bread crumbs, pour over them boiling water and boil till soft, stirring well; take from the fire and gradually stir in a little glycerine or sweet oil, so as to render the poultice pliable when applied.

- HOP POULTICE – Boil one handful of dried hops in half a pint of water, until the half pint is reduced to a gill , then stir into it enough Indian meal to thicken it.

- MUSTARD POULTICE– Into one gill of boiling water stir one tablespoonful of Indian meal; spread the paste thus made upon a cloth and spread over the paste one teaspoonful of mustard flour. It you wish a mild poultice, use a teaspoonful of mustard as it is prepared for the table, instead of the mustard flour.

- Equal parts of ground mustard and flour made into a paste with warm water, and spread between two pieces of muslin, form the indispensable mustard plaster.

- WORMWOOD and ARNICA are sometimes applied in poultices. Steep the herbs in half a pint of cold water and when all their virtue is extracted stir in a little bran or rye meal to thicken the liquid; the herbs must not be removed from the liquid.

68

- GINGER POULTICE -This is made like a mustard poultice, using ground ginger instead of mustard. A little vinegar is sometimes added to each of these poultices.

- STRAMONIUM POULTICE- Stir one tablespoonful of Indian meal into a gill of boiling water and add one tablespoonful of bruised stramonium seeds. This is a useful application for sprains and bruises.

- LINSEED POULTICE – Take four ounces of powdered linseed and gradually sprinkle it into a half pint of hot water.

CAMPHORATED OIL

- Best oil of Lucca, gum camphor. Pound some gum camphor and fill a wide-necked pint bottle one-third full: fill up with olive oil and set away until the camphor is absorbed. Excellent lotion for sore chest, sore throat, aching limbs, etc.

OTHER UNUSUAL REMEDIES AND CURES

- To cure warts, pick dandelions two or three times a day and rub the milky juice from the stems on the warts.

- Young dandelion weeds are iron-rich and are good in salads.

- They're also a mild diuretic and help against urinary infections.

- Mix equal parts of witch hazel and rubbing alcohol and massage tired back or sore muscles.

- Put basil on the skin as an insect repellant.

- Pains in the side are most promptly relieved by the application of mustard.

- Sprains and bruises call for an application of the tincture of arnica.

- For a sprained ankle, the whites of eggs and powdered alum made into a plaster is almost a specific.

- Use old-fashioned horehound drops to soothe a sore throat.

- Eat raw garlic to stop a sneezing fit.

- To destroy the taste of castor oil, beat the castor oil with the white of egg until both are thoroughly mixed.

- *Fainting seems to have been very severe in olden times according to these instructions*—Immediately place the person fainting in a lying position, with head lower than the body. In this way consciousness returns immediately, while in the erect position it often ends in death. (1900's)

- Plants and flowers ought not to be allowed to remain in a chamber at night. Experiments have proved that plants and flowers in the daytime take up carbonic acid gas (the refuse of respiration) and give off oxygen (a gas so necessary and beneficial to health): but give out at night a poisonous exhalation.

NUTRITIONAL RECIPES FROM THE PAST

- CHICKEN PANADA– One cup of cold roasted or boiled chicken, pounded to a paste. Add half a cup of stale bread crumbs, and enough boiling chicken liquor to make one quart. Serve hot a cup at a time.

- HEALTH BREAD, MADE OF ENTIRE WHEAT FLOUR– To

three pints of water add a small cake of yeast and a teaspoonful of salt. Mix with this a sufficient quantity of entire wheat flour to make a soft dough, and mold into baking pans. Let it rise about one-half as much as is usual with other bread before baking. Allowing bread to rise but once increases its nutrition. As the flour is very coarse, making the dough soft allows for swelling. Bake in a hot oven in the same manner as other bread, with the exception that it should be baked a trifle longer.

- RUSK –Bread and crackers may be made into granola by first drying till brown, and then grinding in a coffee or hand mill. This is a very serviceable article for thickening puddings; soups, etc. May be eaten with hot milk.

- GRAHAM CRISPS – Mix graham flour and cold water into a very stiff dough. Knead, roll very thin; and bake quickly in a hot oven. Excellent food for dyspeptics.

- RICE WAFFLES – Take one part of boiled rice to three parts of water, and stir in sufficient graham or whole-wheat flour to make a batter a little thicker than when the flour is used alone. Bake in cast-iron gem-pans; in a very hot oven; though the heat should not be sufficient to brown them in less than fifteen minutes; a longer time toughens the crust. They should be baked on the top first, to prevent the escape of air and steam. The pans should be heated very hot before dripping the batter in. To prevent sticking; smear with sweet-oil or fresh butter, and when thoroughly heated, carefully wipe away as much as possible of the oil.

- OATMEAL BREAKFAST CAKE– Saturate oatmeal of medium fineness with water. Pour the batter into a shallow baking dish, and shake down level. It should be wet enough so that when this is done a little water will stand on the top. Bake twenty minutes in a quick oven. It may also be baked in fifteen minutes on the top of the stove in a covered dish.

- GRAHAM BREAKFAST ROLLS – Make a stiff batter with cold

water, work in as much flour as will knead well, and then knead for twenty minutes or half an hour. Make into rolls one-half inch to to two inches in thickness, and bake in a hot oven on a grate or baking pan dusted with flour, laying them a little distance apart. Excellent rolls may be made by kneading flour into cold graham, oatmeal, or oatmeal pudding.

- SOFT BUISCUIT OR WAFFLES – Take one part of cold soft water stir two parts of graham or whole-wheat flour. Sift slowly in with one hand while stirring with the other, thus endeavoring to get in as much air as possible. If flour made from red wheat is used, a little less water will be required. The batter should be thick enough so that it will not settle flat. It it is too thin, the waffles will be flat and blistered, if too thick, they will be tough and heavy. Bake in cast-iron gem-pans; in a very hot oven; though the heat should not be sufficient to brown them in less than fifteen minutes; a longer time toughens the crust. They should be baked on the top first, to prevent the escape of air and steam. The pans should be heated very hot before dripping the batter in. To prevent sticking; smear with sweet-oil or fresh butter, and when thoroughly heated, carefully wipe away as much as possible of the oil.

- CHICKEN JELLY- Take half a raw chicken, in a coarse cloth and pound till well mashed, bones and meat together. Place the mass in a covered dish with water sufficient to cover it well. Allow it to simmer slowly till the liquor is reduced about one-half and the meat is thoroughly cooked. Press through a fine sieve or cloth, and salt to taste. Place on the stove to simmer about five minutes. When cold, remove all particles of grease.

- LEMON JELLY -Put an ounce of gelatin in a large bowl with four tablespoonfuls of cold water to soften it. When soft, pour over it just three pints of boiling water, add two and a half cups of granulated sugar and the juice of three large lemons. Stir well, and drain through flannel or a very fine strainer. Pour into cups and when cold put into the refrigerator until next day. This is very toothsome, but of no value as a food, and hence useful only in cases in which nourishment is required.

- BREAD JELLY – Pour boiling water over bread crumbs, place the mixture on the fire, and let it boil until it is perfectly smooth. Take it off, and after pouring off the water, flavor with something agreeable, as a little raspberry or currant jelly water. Pour into a mold until required for use.

- SAGE JELLY – Simmer gently in a pint of water two tablespoonfuls of sage until it thickens, frequently stirring. A little sugar may be added if desired.

- TAPIOCA MILK – Put an ounce of best tapioca into a pint and a quarter of fresh milk, and let it simmer gently for two hours and fifteen minutes; stirring frequently. Sweeten to taste.

- BRAN TEA – Take three tablespoonfuls of bran (not very coarse) and put it in a jug. Add to it one quart of boiling water, cover the jug, and allow the mixture to stand for half an hour. Strain and sweeten to taste.

- RICE WATER – Put three ounces of good rice into a quart of boiling water, and let it boil for an hour. Strain, sweeten, and flavor with a little lemon.

- APPLE AND TOAST WATER – Peel and quarter a pound of sub-acid apples, bake them, and put them in a jar; add half a pound of sugar, and a piece of bread toasted until it is dark brown; then pour a gallon of boiling water over them, and leave them to cool. When cold, press through a colander. A quarter of a pound of pearl barley added instead the bread is very good. It should boil for an hour to cook the barley.

- TAMARIND WATER – Take two ounces of tamarinds and one-fourth of a pound of stoned raisins; boil them in a quart and a half of water for an hour; strain and when cold it is ready for use.

- CURRANT WATER – Take the juice of one pound of fresh currants and a few raspberries, one-half a pound of granulated sugar and a gallon of cold water; stir till mixed well.

- TOAST WATER – Brown a few crusts a nice, deep brow, but do not allow to blacken or burn. Break into small pieces, and put into a jar. Pour over the pieces a quart of boiling water; cover the jar and let the mixture remain until cold. When strained, it will be ready for use.

- LEMONADE – Mix the slices and juice of two lemons with three spoonfuls of refined sugar; and add a pint of cold or iced water.

- HOT LEMONADE – Take two thin slices and the juice of one lemon; mix with two tablespoonfuls of granulated sugar, and add one-half pint of boiling water.

- FLAXSEED LEMONADE – To four tablespoonfuls of whole flaxseed add a quart of boiling water, and let it steep three hours; then add the juice of two lemons; sweeten to the taste, and then with cold water. Drink cold.

- BARLEY WATER -Take half a teacupful of good pearl barley. First wash it thoroughly; then boil five or ten minutes in fresh water. Drain off this water and pour on two quarts of boiling water and boil down to one quart. Flavor if desired with a little lemon or sugar. Thin to required consistency with boiling water.

- GUM ARABIC WATER – Put an ounce of choice gum arabic into a jar with tow ounces of refined sugar and a pint of water. Place the jar in a sauce-pan of warm water and stir until dissolved. Add a little lemon to flavor. This is a good drink for consumptives.

- FLAXSEED TEA -Take an ounce of whole flaxseed, half an ounce of crushed licorice root, an ounce of refined sugar, and four tablespoonfuls of lemon juice. Pour over these ingredients a quart of boiling water; let this stand near the fire for four hours, and then strain off the liquid. The flaxseed should not be crushed, as the mucilage is in the outer part of the kernel and if bruised the boiling water will extract the oil of the seed and render the decoction nauseous. The tea should be made fresh daily.

- BRAN OR WHEAT COFFEE – Mix bran and molasses to a stiff paste, spread on a tin and brown in the oven. Brown wheat in the same way. Be careful not to allow the heat to be sufficient to burn or scorch. Use as other coffee, for which it is a good and unstimulating substitute. Wheat coffee is sometimes sold at the stores in packages.

- WHITE OF EGG AND MILK – The white of an egg beaten to a stiff froth and stirred very quickly into a glass of milk is a very nourishing food for persons whose digestion is weak, also for children who cannot digest milk alone. The white of egg has a tendency to prevent the formation of hard curds in the stomach.

DISHES FOR THE INVALID

- TOAST WATER- Toast slightly a piece of bread and add to it boiling water, if preferred sweeten. It may be flavored with lemon or orange peel.

- BARLEY COFFEE – Roast barley until well brown and boil a tablespoonful of it in a pint of water for five minutes, strain and add a little sugar, if desired. A nourishing drink toward the close of fever and during convalescence.

- OATMEAL COFFEE – Mix common oatmeal and water to form cake; bake and brown it, powder it, and boil in water five minutes. Good for checking obstinate vomiting, especially in cholera morbus

- FARINA GRUEL – One tablespoonful Hecker's farina, one teaspoonful salt, one cup boiling water, one of milk. Cook all together except the milk, for fifteen minutes, or until it thickens, then add the milk and boil again. Farina is a preparation of wheat and very healthful.

- CRACKER GRUEL – Four tablespoonfuls powdered cracker, one cup boiling water, one cup of milk, and a little salt. Boil up once and serve fresh.

- EGG GRUEL – The yolk of one egg beaten well, one teaspoonful sugar, one cup hot milk, white of egg beaten to a foam. Flavor with nutmeg or lemon. Good for cold if taken very hot before retiring.

- SLIPPERY ELM TEA – Pour one cup hot water over one teaspoonful of powdered slippery elm bark, or on a piece of the fresh bark. When cool, strain through wire strainer and flavor with very little lemon. Add a little sugar. This is soothing for inflamed mucous surfaces.

- ACID FRUIT DRINKS – Poor boiling water on mashed cranberries, barberries, whortleberries or cherries. When cold, strain and sweeten as desired. No. 2. - Stir a tablespoonful of any acid jelly or fruit syrup into a tumbler of ice water. No. 3. - Dissolve one tablespoonful cream of tartar in one pint of water. Sweeten to taste.

- APPLE TEA – Roast two large, sour apples, cover with boiling water. When cool, pour water off, strain and sweeten to taste.

MEAT DISHES FOR THE INVALID

"The majority of mankind believe animal food to be a necessary constituent of the diet. We therefore give a few formulas for the best preparation of meats for the sick. Every particle of fat, skin and membrane must be removed." (1900)

- BEEF TEA – Take a pound of lean beef, cut it fine, put it in a bottle corked tightly, and put the bottle into a kettle of warm water; the water should be allowed to boil for a considerable time; the bottle should then be removed, and the contents poured out. The tea may be salted a little, and a teaspoonful given each time.

  Another way of preparing it is as follows:
  Take a thick steak, broil slightly on a gridiron until the juices have started, and then squeeze thoroughly with a lemon squeezer. The juice thus extracted will be highly nutritious.

- BROILED BEEF PULP – Scrape raw beef to a pulp, make into small cakes and broil as steak, Season with salt and a little cayenne pepper.

- MUTTON BROTH – To make it quickly for an invalid, chop one pound of lean, juicy mutton very fine. Pour over it one pint of cold water, let it stand until the water is red, then heat slowly, simmering ten minutes. Strain, season, and add two tablespoonfuls of soft boiled rice, or thicken slightly with rice flour wet with cold water. Serve warm."

MISCELLANEOUS FOODS FOR THE INVALID

- BRAIN FOOD– Wet one cup of entire wheat flour in a little cold water and stir into one quart of salted boiling water. Cook over hot fire one to two hours. Eat hot or cold. With sugar and cream.

- RICE JELLY – Two tablespoonfuls rice, one quart cold water, salt and sugar to taste. Pick over and wash the rice and cook in water one hour, or until the rice is dissolved. Add a little salt and sugar to taste. If desired for jelly, add lemon juice and strain into a mold. When cold, serve with sugar and cream. If to be used as a drink, add more hot water, making a thin liquid and boil longer with a half square of stick cinnamon. Strain, and serve hot or cold. Rice is good in diarrhea and dysentery, being easily digested and assimilated.

- TAPIOCA JELLY – One-fourth cup pearl tapioca, one pint cold water, one tablespoonful lemon juice, one heaping tablespoonful sugar, salt to taste. Pick over and wash the tapioca, add the cold water, and cook in a double boiler until entirely dissolved. Then add the salt, lemon juice and sugar. Turn into a mold, and when cold, serve with sugar and cream. Half cup strawberry, blackberry or raspberry jam, or currant jelly, may be used instead of lemon, without loss of quality.

- IRISH MOSS JELLY – One half cup Irish moss, one pint boiling water, one lemon, one-third cup of sugar. Soak the moss in cold water until soft, pick over and wash again, then put into the boiling water and simmer until dissolved. Add lemon juice and sugar, and strain into a mold. Currant jelly, instead of lemon, is good, or four or five figs steeped with moss is excellent. The use of sea and Iceland moss is recommended in rheumatic diseases, as they contain bromine and iodine.

- RESTORATIVE JELLY – One-half box gelatine, one cup port wine, one tablespoonful powdered gum arabic, two tablespoonfuls lemon juice, three tablespoonfuls sugar, two cloves. Put all these ingredients together in a glass jar and cover closely. Place the jar on a trivet in a kettle of cold water, heat slowly and the mixture will dissolve. Stir well and strain. Pour into a shallow dish and when cool, cut into small squares. Good for aged or weak persons.

OTHER CURES

- Spinach has a direct effect upon complaints of the kidneys; the common dandelion, used as greens, is excellent for the same trouble; asparagus purifies the blood; celery acts admirably upon the nervous system, and is a cure for rheumatism and neuralgia; tomatoes act upon the liver; beets and turnips are excellent appetizers; lettuce and cucumbers are cooling in their effects upon the system; beans area a very nutritious and strengthening vegetable; while onions, garlic, leeks, chives and shallots, all of which are similar, possess medicinal virtues of a marked character, stimulating the circulatory system, and the consequent increase of the saliva and the gastric juice promoting digestion.

- A drink of hot, strong lemonade before going to bed will often break a cold and cure a sore throat.

- Tickling in the throat is best relieved by a gargling of salt and water.

- A flannel dipped in boiling water and sprinkled with turpentine, laid on the chest as quickly as possible, will relieve the most severe cold and hoarseness.

- Another simple, pleasant remedy is furnished by beating up the white of one egg, adding to it the juice of one lemon, and sweetening with white sugar to taste. Take a teaspoonful from time to time. It has been known to effectually cure the ailment.

- Or bake a lemon or sour orange twenty minutes in a moderate oven. When done, open at one end and take out the inside. Sweeten with sugar or molasses. This is an excellent remedy for hoarseness.

VINEGAR OF THE FOUR THIEVES President Thomas Jefferson's Recipe -1880s

There are interesting stories about this recipe. One of the most popular is that it is a cure for bubonic plague.

The story goes that four thieves who had safely ransacked empty plague-ridden houses and were brought before the French judges in Marseilles. The judges wondered aloud how the thieves avoided becoming sick with the plague. One of the prisoners said, " We drink and wash with this vinegar preparation every few hours," The judges released the prisoners in exchange for the recipe.

Below is President Thomas Jefferson's Recipe for Vinegar of the Four Thieves. The recipe was"well known in colonial Virginia households" and was probably brought by Thomas Jefferson from France in 1794. He was a painstaking collector of everything of practical value.

- Take lavender, rosemary, sage, wormwood (of the tarragon family), rue and mint, of each a large handful; put them in a pot of earthenware, pour on them 4 quarts of very strong vinegar. Cover pot closely and put a board on the top; keep it in the hottest sun 2 weeks. Then strain and bottle, putting in each bottle a clove of garlic. When it has settled in the bottle and become clear pour it off gently; do this until you get it all free from sediment. The proper time to make it is when the herbs are full of vigor, in June. This vinegar is very refreshing in crowded rooms, in the apartments of the sick and is peculiarly grateful when sprinkled about the house in damp weather.

HUMOROUS ANECDOTE

Doctors must have found it difficult sometimes when giving medical instructions to the uneducated. The following anecdote reveals this...

A Well Treated Thermometer

A prominent physician of Baltimore tells of an amusing experience of the early days of his practice when he was residing in a small town where by far the majority of the workers were miners.

I was greatly distressed at the unsanitary conditions prevailing in their cottages, says the doctor, and, among other things, I tried to explain to each household the importance of maintaining a wholesome atmosphere in their sleeping rooms. I laid in a stock of thermometers, which were distributed to the household where they were most needed. I took pains to point out to each family in turn just how this thermometer would indicate the proper degree of temperature.

As I was making the rounds one day I inquired of the woman at the head of one establishment, wherein I observed my thermometer proudly displayed at the end of a string, whether she had followed my instructions

"Yes sir,' answered she; "I'm very careful about the temperature, I watch the thing all the time as it hangs up there."

"What do you do when the temperature rises above us?"

"I take it down sir, an' put it outside till it cools off a bit."
(from Harper's Weekly 1908)

THE GOOD OLE DAYS

MISCELLANEOUS TIPS FROM THE PAST

- REMEBERING DATES- It's easy to remember anniversaries and special days with a greeting if you select all your cards at one time. Address the envelopes and and index them according to the date they should be mailed.

- HOW TO MAKE A STRAW BROOM - Collect the straw any time during the winter after it has shed its blooms. Strip off the blades up to about 15 inches from the bottom of the handle. Give it a good shaking to get rid of any remaining blooms. Take a bundle of straw about 2 inches in diameter, spread the ends you plan to use for a handle on waxed paper and give them a good coat of waterproof glue. Make sure that the glue touches each straw at some point. Wind a cord tightly around the straw, about 15 inches from the end, about a dozen times or more to make a band 3/4 inches wide. Then move 3 or 4 inches down the handle and make another. Repeat the bands until you reach the end. Fasten the cord by weaving back and forth between the straw. When thoroughly dry, shellac the handle.

- CUTTING GLASS BOTTLES FOR CUPS AND JARS - A simple, practical way is to take a red-hot poker with a pointed end; make a mark with a file to begin the cut; then apply the hot iron and a crack will start, which will follow the iron wherever it is carried. This is, on the whole, simple, and better than the use of strings wet with turpentine, etc."

- CURE CATS FROM CATCHING CHICKENS - To cure cats catching chickens: when a cat is seen to catch chickens, tie one of them around her neck and make her wear it for two or three days. Fasten it securely, for she will make incredible efforts to get rid of it. Be firm for that time, and the cat is permanently cured; she will never again touch a chick. (From a 1900 publication)

- CURE DOG FROM EATING EGGS - To cure a dog of eating eggs, blow an ordinary hen's egg, expelling the entire contents. Stop up one end of the shell with wax, then fill it from the other end of the shell with strong spirits of ammonia, or "Hartshorn." Seal that end and then put it where the dog can get it. If he crushes it, he will never be desirous of repeating the luxury of egg eating. After the dog has had one ammoniacal feast, a little of the fluid poured into the nest will remind him of the fact that he once was burnt, and also will serve to cleanse the nest of vermin.

HOW CHILDREN SHOULD BEHAVE (1937 rules)

- Always greet the members of your family when you enter and always bid them goodbye when you leave.

- Always rise to a standing position when visitors enter, and greet them after your elders.

- Never address a visitor until he has started the conversation unless he is a person of your own age or younger.

- Never interrupt a conversation. Wait until the party talking has finished.

- Always rise when your visitor or your elders stand.

- Never let your mother or your father bring you a chair or get one for themselves. Wait on them instead of being waited on.

OFFICE RULES AND REGULATIONS BY GEIGER, 1872

- Office employees will daily sweep the floors, dust the furniture, shelves, and showcases.
- Each day fill lamps, clean chimneys, and trim wicks. Wash the windows once a week.

- Each clerk will bring in a bucket of water and a scuttle of coal for the day's business.

- Make your pens carefully. You may whittle nibs to your individual taste.

- This office will open at 7 a.m. and close at 8 p. m. daily except on the Sabbath, on which day it will remain closed.

- Men employees will be given an evening off each week for courting purposes, or two evenings a week if they go regularly to church.

- Every employee should lay aside from each pay a goodly sum of his earnings for his benefits during his declining, so that he will not become a burden upon the charity of his betters.

- Any employee who smokes Spanish cigars, uses liquor in any form, gets shaved at a barber shop, or frequents pool or public halls will give a good reason to suspect his worth, intentions, integrity and honesty.

- The employee who has performed his labor faithfully and without faults for a period of five years in my service and who has been thrifty and attentive to his religious duties and is looked upon by his fellow men as a substantial and law-abiding citizen will be given an increase of five cents per day, providing a just return of profits from the business permits it.

DID YOU KNOW?

- Dates in United States colonial times often indicated the month by a number instead of its name, because most of the months had pagan names. These names were unacceptable to the Puritans and Quakers. The Quakers, along with everyone else in England and the American colonies did not use the Gregorian calendar until 1732 so in using Old Quaker records, until 1732, the "1st mo" is March.

- In colonial times, hair was generally worn up, off the face. Letting hair down was considered risque. Neck-length side curls were allowed, and special locks of ringlets to be worn under hats were available in the latter periods. In the early period hair might be dressed on pie-shaped forms seen in Elizabethan portraits. In the mid-seventeenth century ringlets were fashionable.

- Although ladies wore high, cylindrical wigs in the 1770s in Europe, they were a rare occurrence in the colonies, occurring mostly in the larger, more cosmopolitan cities such as Philadelphia and Charles Town. They were almost always case for comment. Such wigs were rarely taken off, even at night, and setting mouse and louse traps in them was not unheard of. Calash bonnets, worn in the very late period and made popular by the high wig styles, were made with a collapsing wire framework extending the sides in front of the face.

- In the seventeenth century, a person's social standing determined what he or she ate at dinners? The best food was placed next to the most important people. Also, people didn't tend to sample everything that was on the table, they just ate what was closest to them.

- In the seventeenth century people weren't served their meals individually. Foods were served onto the table and then people took the food from the table and ate it. All the servers had to do was move the food from the place where it was cooked onto the table. People ate with spoons, knives, and their fingers. They wiped their hands on large cloth napkins which they also used to pick up hot morsels of food.
- The wealthy had slate floors that would get slippery in the winter when wet, so they spread thresh (straw) on the floor to help keep their footing. As the winter wore on, they kept adding more thresh until when you opened the door it would all start slipping outside. A piece of wood was placed in the entranceway. Hence the saying a "thresh hold."

ONE HUNDRED YEARS AGO

- Only 14 percent of the homes in the U.S. had a bathtub.

- More than 95 percent of all births in the U.S. took place at home.

- The average wage in the U.S. was 22 cents per hour.

- The average U.S. worker made $200 - $400 per year.

- Only 8 percent of the homes had a telephone.

- A three-minute call from Denver to New York City cost $11.00

- Sugar cost four cents a pound.

- Eggs cost fourteen cents a dozen.

- Coffee cost fifteen cents a pound.

Additional Books by Donna R. Causey can be found on her websites:

www.alabamapioneers.com

www.daysgoneby.me

Follow Donna R. Causey on FACEBOOK

http://www.facebook.com/ribbonoflove

http://www.facebook.com/alabamapioneers

http://www.facebook.com/daygonebyme

and contact her via her

Author's Page on Amazon.com

TAPESTRY OF LOVE SERIES

by

Donna R. Causey

RIBBON OF LOVE – Book one

FAITH AND COURAGE - Book two

FREEHEARTS – Book Three

New Series

THE COTTINGHAMS

THE INHERITANCE – Book one

RIBBON OF LOVE

by

Donna R. Causey

My life is but a weaving
Between my Lord and me...
I may not choose the colors;
He knows what they should be;
For He can view the pattern
Upon the upper side,
While I can see it only
on this, the under side.
Sometimes He weaveth sorrow,
Which seemth strange to me;
But I will trust His judgment
And work on faithfully.
"Tis He who fills the shuttle;
He knows just what is best;
So I shall weave in earnest
And leave with Him the rest.
Not till the loom is silent
And the shuttles cease to fly,
Shall God unroll the canvas
And explain the reason why
The dark threads are as needful,
In the weaver's skillful hand,
As the treads of gold and silver
In the pattern He has planned.

Unknown

CHAPTER ONE

June 30, 1637, London, England

Dr. Henry Pattenden was fairly secluded as he stood in the shade of a yard goods shop. But he still felt uneasy about his position as he warily studied the crowd in London's market square.

It's probably not safe for me to be here, but how could I stay away? Dr. Bastwick was my mentor.

The day was already stifling hot and the dusty streets were full of excited people. The extreme congestion resulted in frequent disagreements and disturbances within the crowd. Children dashed about, stirred clouds of dust, and nearly toppled adults as they darted in their play—unaware of the import of the day.

Sudden shouts rang out near the center of the street and Dr. Pattenden's attention was drawn toward two boys involved in an altercation.

"Ye pushed first," the taller boy shouted defiantly as the stared down at a younger child who was clutching his knee in obvious pain. The taller boys' fists were curled. He was ready to continue the fight.

Blood flowed from the smaller boy's lips and he screamed,"Me didn't. Ye did!"

Two women in plain dress stopped their conversation and stared at the boys a moment. Then the grey-haired woman spoke to the younger woman and in unison they walked with deliberation toward the two boys. The grey-haired woman yanked the taller boy up by his ear while the other woman bent down and examined the younger boy's knee.

"Owwww, Mum! Ye'll pull me ear off."

"And ye'll deserve it!" his mother retorted loudly. "How's ya youngun?"

"Not much harm done, a scratch on his knee—this cut lip is bleeding some," the younger woman replied as she dabbed at her son's lip with a handkerchief. "Best we return home and clean it up. "That's the end of excitement today. for thee."

Her son stopped wailing and gave two loud sniffs. "Nay, Mum, 'tis okay. See—the bleeding's stopped." He pushed her hand away and gave a quick swipe across his mouth with the back of his hand, smearing blood and staining his cheeks bright red.

"Stopped, 'eh, that was quick." She gave the other woman a wink. "Mayhaps we'll remain longer—if ya promise not to run or fight."

She looked up at the other woman and smiled, "Have you ever seen anyone heal so fast?"

Before she could answer, the younger boy pushed himself up from the ground and attempted to run off. His mother caught his arm. "Wait, son. Ya need to be cleaned up a bit."

With a firm grip on his left arm, she pulled him toward the water trough near the shop where Pattenden stood. He gave the woman a brief nod; she nodded back, and then bent over the trough. Then she wet the corner of her apron in the water and attended to her son.

The older woman remained in the street with her hands placed firmly on her hips. She frowned at her son. He glanced toward some boys playing marbles on the edge of the street behind his mother. All at once, she reached out, caught his chin in her hand, and lowered her face to his eye level. She scowled at him and her angry words rose above the street noise.

"Stay out of fights today of all days. There's enough mischief happening without ya adding to it."

"Aw Mum," the boy whined as he wrestled to free himself from her tight grasp. Finally, he broke away and ran toward the boys playing marbles. He shouted back, "He started it!"

The old woman watched him flee. "That's what ya always say. Always someone else's fault—not thine," she muttered, "You'll be the death of me yet."

Henry watched the woman shade her eyes with one hand as she looked toward the New Palace Yard. She gave a heavy sigh and squinted at the stark, wooden scaffold standing in the street. A pillory stood squarely in the middle of the platform.

Even though it was a miserably hot day, the old woman gave a shiver and pulled her ragged shawl tighter around her shoulders. Then, in an obvious attempt to avoid the dung and muck in the street, she lifted the skirt of her tattered dress and ambled gingerly over to a group of similarly clad women near Pattenden.

When the old woman drew near Dr. Pattenden, he overheard her growl, "There's enough trouble happening today, that's for sure."

The women greeted her warmly and nodded at her comment. Most of the women in the group were dressed in long aprons which covered their bodices and skirts. Their hair was completely hidden under small lace fringed rochets. Some of the women chatted and rocked infants in their arms while toddlers clung to their mother's long skirts.

Henry looked toward the scaffold and studied it for a few minutes. A post stood in the center with three stocks radiating out like spokes in a wheel. The stocks had holes where the head and hands of men could be confined. It would truly be an instrument of torture if the crowd participated by throwing objects at prisoners.

Suddenly an argument broke out between two burly men near him. Several other men rushed over and pulled them apart before a fist fight ensued.

The streets became increasingly packed with people. Henry withdrew further in the shadows and anxiously watched the crowd.

Few seemed intent on trading. Several men near him were engrossed in a solemn conversation.

Most of the men on the street were dressed in plain jerkins with short leather breeches, and they had grim expressions on their faces. Others cast furtive glances around as if expecting trouble.

Sprinkled among the mass of people like bright flowers on a dry dusty field, were clusters of colorfully attired men and women.

They conversed in loud voices, and laughed uproariously at a humorous remark as if they were attending a party. The women beside them wore elegantly brocaded dresses in bright colors. Starched collars, tight fitting bodices with ruffles trimmed their tiny waists.

The morning wore on and the hot sun beat down so Henry stretched his arms, removed his coat and placed it neatly over his arm. What had been a quiet murmuring in the crowd, was gradually changing. Loud shouts penetrated the drone of conversation.

A very inebriated man shouted above the crowd noise, "Me thinks it's about time something was done about them. They've been allowed free rein in their writing too long, whilst we take the brunt of the suffering."

Ayes, and Nays filled the air as the people agreed or disagreed with the drunken man.

Buoyed by the response from the crowd, the drunk became more animated and he jumped on a crate to continue his tirade. "Me say let's hang 'um all, they be just trouble makers anyway."

Before he could continue, a couple of men with strong muscular arms, grabbed him by the shirt collar and threw him to the ground. "Go home ya old drunk," one of the man shouted. "Ya don't know what ye're talking about."

The penitent man crawled off to the side and disappeared in the crowd.

A bench in front of a shop across the street was empty so Henry walked over and sat down, but he continued to survey the crowd for danger.

Families drifted in from the outlying countryside and the mass of people swelled and overflowed into the side streets. Whole families seemed intent on watching the spectacle. The overwhelming smell of fish, poultry, overripe produce, and other food mixed with the stink of dung and waste permeated the air.

Restless from waiting, Henry stood again and moved closer to the scaffold near the center of the street. He smiled at a small child about four-years of age, who was holding her father's hand. She held a doll in her other hand which trailed in the dusty street behind her.

All at once, the loud tramp of horses' hooves was heard and people pushed against each other to get out of their way. Amidst the chaos, someone stepped on the young girl's doll, and it was ripped from her small hands. The doll lay in the middle of the street directly in the path of the oncoming horses. Distraught over her lost, the child screamed, "Wait, Papa!" Then she released her grip from her father's hand and ran toward the center of the street to retrieve the doll. Soldiers on horseback appeared at the same instant only a few yards away from where she was standing.

Henry watched in horror as the horses bore down on the spot where the child stood stark still in obvious panic. The horses pounded the ground and headed straight toward her as she screamed, "Papa! Papa!"

Her father frantically searched at the back of the crowd for his screaming child. Henry saw the potential tragedy unfolding before his eyes and reacted quickly. He rushed into the street, grabbed hold of the child's pinafore, and pulled the young girl to safety just seconds before she would have been crushed by the horses' hooves.

The child's grateful father rushed to them and collected his daughter. The little girl whimpered as she clasped her father's neck tightly. The man shook Henry's hand and said, "Thank ye! Thank ye friend!"

"Aye, you'd have done the same. Glad to help." Then Henry saw some foot soldiers circulating among the people behind the man. He turned away and tried to fade within the mass of people.

After the horse soldiers passed down the street, a hush fell over the crowd. Only the loud creak of cart wheels penetrated the silence. A horse-drawn cart suddenly appeared, and the people along the street started pushing en masse toward the cart. Soon the cart was unable to move forward due to the number of people surrounding it.

Soldiers promptly responded. With swords drawn, they forced

men, women and children to separate until a narrow path was created The cart driver threaded the cart through the mass of people, and continued toward its destination, the New Palace Yard.

"They got ye now!" shouted a man in the crowd. "Now ye'll see how it feels," he continued. His jeer was isolated among the silent shock of onlookers. Only pockets of quiet mumbling could be heard.

Three men stood on the bed of the cart with their arms chained to the sides of the wagon. The rolling prison drew past three boys standing beside a pile of stones they had collected for the occasion. One boy shouted, "Heretic", and he threw a large rock at a man in the cart. The rock hit a prisoner's cheek and he flinched a moment, but continued to stare straight ahead. The prisoner was William Prynne, a prominent barrister of Lincoln's Inn.

All at once, a barrage of rocks, vegetables and debris flew through the air at the men in the wagon. The prisoners lowered their heads and tried to dodge the pelting.

Henry grimaced when a stone hit Dr. Bastwick's forehead and blood flowed from the deep gash. Dr. John Bastwick was a kind gentleman. He was educated at the esteemed Emmanuel College and was Henry's mentor. Bastwick had taken a keen interest in Henry and taught him everything he knew about medicine.

Reverend Henry Burton, a Puritan divine stood behind Dr. Bastwick in the wagon.

All three men had been found guilty of sedition by the Star Chamber conducted by Bishop Laud. Their punishment was to be pilloried and their ears cut off in front of the populace. The Star Chamber created a sensation in England when they ordered the highly unusual punishment for the three prominent men. Such savage punishment was not typically given to distinguished gentlemen.

Fights broke out among the mob around the cart as some men attempted to stop the rock throwers. Henry was thankful to see that the usual barrage of mockery and abuse directed at prisoners was wanting. Instead, the three men seemed to command respect among the majority of onlookers midst their humiliation.

The cart reached the scaffold and the soldiers unchained the prisoners' arms from the sides of the wagon. The soldiers did not see four young maidens making their way closer to the platform. A whisper was heard and then a few people moved aside to make a path for the young girls. Four maidens darted forward and threw herbs and flowers on the path in front of the prisoners. Then they quickly retreated and were swallowed up within the congregation of people before the guards could react. The soldiers kicked angrily at the flowers as they pulled and half drug the prisoners to the scaffold.

Pyrnne ascended the ladder to the platform first. A rock flew toward him, but missed and ricocheted off the post and hit the executioner instead.

"Good shot!" someone shouted. People in the crowd laughed. The soldiers searched the mass of people to discover the perpetrator.

The interlude allowed Bastwick's wife to grasp her husband's face as he passed and kiss the ears that were about to be cut off.

A soldier roughly pushed her aside. Henry shouted along with the angry crowd at the harsh treatment of Baswick's wife by the soldier.

Bastwick looked back at her as he climbed the ladder and said, "Don't be frightened."

"Farewell, my dearest, be of comfort, I am not dismayed," she replied.

The guard shoved Dr. Bastwick across the platform. The guards that remained on the ground completely surrounded Reverend Burton. He made his way to the ladder with no further disruption.

It was the custom that prisoners were allowed to speak before their sentences were executed and Pyrnne, the barrister, spoke first. Silence fell as everyone strained to hear his voice. Pyrnne repeated a great part of the court's proceedings at first. Then he cited two statues against libeling the Queen that had been enacted during the reigns of Queen Mary and Queen Elizabeth.

"In these instances, the offender being lawfully convicted by verdict, his own confession, or by the oaths of two sufficient witnesses—witnesses brought face to face at his trial, should have both his ears cut off, unless he paid 100£ within one month, and should suffer three months for payment, and suffer six months, imprisonment."

"I challenge ye, look at the times of Queen Mary and Queen Elizabeth, and the times now of King Charles and how far more dangerous it is now to write against a bishop or two, than against a king or queen."

Shouts of acclamation rang out.

He continued, "The most there was during Queen Mary and Queen Elizabeth's time was but six months imprisonment in ordinary prisons. And the delinquent might redeem his ears for 200£, and had two months time for payment, but no fine, while here today we are fined 5000£ a piece, to be perpetually imprisoned in the remotest castles, where no friends permitted and to lose our ears without redemption."

Cheers bellowed from the crowd. Soon the New Palace Yard was thundering with shouts of approbation.

Encouraged, Pyrnne pressed on, "Then there was no stigmatization; here we must be branded on both cheeks—then a legal conviction was requisite, here all to be taken *pro confesso* without verdict, confession, or so much as one witness! If the people knew what times they had been cast and what changes of laws, religions, and ceremonies had been made by one man, they would look upon them. If they look upon them—the people might see that no degree or profession was exempt from the prelates' malice—for here is a divine for the soul, a physician for the body, and a lawyer for the estates. and the next to be censured in the Star Chamber is likely to be a bishop! If all the martyrs that suffered in Queen Mary's days are called fanatical heretics, factious fellows, traitors and rebels, condemned by the Holy Church, what can we look for?"

The people became more and more vocal in their affirmation and the executioner sensed trouble.

"Place him in the stocks," he commanded.

The guards quickly followed his orders. The executioner raised the top board to bind Pyrnne's head. He scowled as he noted a problem. Pyrnne had previously been punished by the Star Chamber and both of his ears were cut off at the time. Though an obvious attempt had been made to sew the ears back on, clearly only stumps remained.

Someone shouted, "Me hope Archbishop Laud won't be too disappointed since Pyrnne has no ears to cut off." Laughter thundered among the crowd.

Once Pyrnne was encased in the stocks, the executioner moved to secure Bastwick. He started to speak, but the executioner ordered him to stop. Pyrnne continued his discourse.

"Silence!" barked, the executioner. "Nail his ears to the stocks!"

The guards obeyed. Tears filled Pyrnne's eyes, but he did not flinch or shout out as they completed the gruesome task.

Next, Reverend Burton was brought to the platform and roughly bound by the guards.

A few people gathered next to the scaffold near Reverend Burton. One man with a red beard asked, "Is the pillory not uneasy for ye neck and shoulders?"

Reverend Burton replied, "How can Christ yoke be uneasy? He bears the heavier end and I bear the lighter; and if mine were too heavy, he would bear that too."

The crowd cheered. After all three men were securely encased in the stocks, the executioner stood in the center of the platform and read aloud:

"The following named men are hereby convicted of the crime of sedition by the Court of High Commission: William Prynne, barrister, Dr. John Bastwick and Reverend Henry Burton. They are condemned to stand not less than two hours in the pillory, amputation of both ears and to pay severally a fine of 5000£ to the king and to be imprisoned for life."

After reading the order a guard nailed the charge to the center post of the pillory.

The executioner returned to Pyrnne and paused to decide what to do about his ears.

Prynne calmly said, "Come friend—on with it. I fear not for Christ sustains me."

Clearly angered by his comment, the executioner swung his sword at the right stump of his ear. Blood spurted on the executioner and formed rivulets on the platform. Pyrnne appeared dazed for a moment but remained steady. Then the executioner cut the left stump so close that he took away a piece of Pyrnne's cheek. Blood stained the platform under Pyrnne and poured onto the ground below. A few men hissed and threw rotten vegetables and rocks at the executioner, but halted when the soldiers rushed into the crowd.

Henry retreated to the back of the crowd.

Discouraged by Pyrnne's response, the executioner moved on to cut off Bastwick's ears. With a sharp swing, he sliced the right ear off and in another swing he hacked at the left ear. A massive amount of blood flowed onto the scaffold and a groan swelled up from the people. A piece of Bastwick's left ear dangled against his cheek.

Bastwick was dazed for a brief moment. Finally, he regained his composure and shouted with an anguished voice, "If I had a thousand lives, I would give them up for the cause."

Some confusion was taking place near the ladder. Henry looked toward the ladder and he saw Bastwick's wife climb onto the platform. Then she darted past the guards and rushed toward her husband. She knelt down before him and picked up his ears. The executioner reacted and shoved her against the floor. He almost pushed her off the platform.

Henry joined in the roar that bellowed from the mob at her cruel treatment.

A guard grabbed her arm, but she shoved him away and proudly stood by herself. With a hand stained from her husband's bloody ears, she pushed aside a lock of her curly brown hair from her eyes, turned slowly and walked stoically toward the ladder amid shouts of approval from the crowd. When she reached the edge of the platform tears flowed from her eyes, clouding her vision. She wiped at them with her blood stained hand. Her tears mingled with her husband's blood and drops were visible on her dress. She slowly descended each rung and fell to the ground in tears. A group of ladies quickly gathered around to console her.

The executioner was clearly frustrated at this point. He drew his sword high above his head and with one swift down stroke sliced off Reverend Burton's right ear. The cut was so close to his head that his temporal artery was opened. Blood gushed out in a strong spurt, splattering the executioner's chest. With another stroke, he cut off the other ear. Blood flowed to the platform and formed a pool of red beneath the divine's head. Drips of blood penetrated the platform, staining the ground below.

For a moment Reverend Burton appeared faint. But he regained his strength and exclaimed, "Christ is a good Master, and worth suffering for! If the world would but know his goodness and had tasted his sweetness; all would come and be his servants!"

Shouts of agreement roared from the crowd.

Next a hot iron was brought to the scaffold with the letters S. L. engraved on them, for the crime of sedition. Pyrnne taunted the executioner, "Come friend, come, burn me—cut me! I have learned to fear the fire of hell and not what man can do unto me, Come; scar me—scar me!"

"Nay, ye need worry not, ye shall have what's ya due," laughed the executioner. Then he looked at the iron and exclaimed, "This iron has grown cold, fire it again. This scoundrel wants fire!"

The iron was reheated and returned red hot to the executioner. He grabbed it and pressed the glowing implement of torture against Prynne's right cheek. He left it there for an excruciating long time. The stench of cooking flesh filled the air and some ladies in the crowd covered their noses with handkerchiefs to block the suffocating odor.

"The punishment was to brand him, not cook 'em!" shouted a burly man near the pillory.

The executioner, now visibly excited by the crowd's adverse reaction, revealed a menacing smile. Then he twisted and pressed the instrument of torment harder against Prynne's cheek.

Tears of anguish flowed from Prynne's eyes, still he did not cry out in pain. At last, the executioner finally withdrew the iron. Pyrnne exclaimed, "The more I am beaten down, the more I am lifted up."

Disgusted, the executioner barked to a waiting soldier, "The fire grows cold. Heat it again!"

The iron was reheated and returned to the executioner's waiting hand. "Let's see how ye like this one," the executioner barked with a smirk on his face.

Again, he pressed the iron on Pyrnne's left cheek where the skin had been ripped away. Tears flowed from Pyrnne's eyes as he continued to stare straight ahead. Ironically, the hot iron staunched the flow of blood from his cheek.

The iron was heated again and the executioner pressed it against Bastwick's cheek. A whimper came from the crowd and a soldier on the platform pointed to Bastwick's wife. The executioner turned toward her and grinned. He ordered the iron fired again. Then he thrust it hard against Bastwick's other cheek. It made a sizzling noise like bacon frying on a skillet.

A collective groan came from the assemblage. Henry turned his back to the scaffold. His face was ashen.

The executioner laughed and exclaimed, "Where is ya Christ now?"

Bastick's wife began to wail.

Bastwick closed his eyes for a minute, then he opened them and said, "Sweet wife, be of good cheer! Christ sustains me."

The executioner threw the iron at a soldier to reheat it. When it was returned, he pressed it against the left cheek of Reverend Burton. Finally, the executioner branded Reverend Burton's right cheek without reheating the iron.

The divine shouted, "Christ is a Good Master, I gladly suffer for thee!"

His duty completed, the frustrated executioner climbed down the ladder from the platform. He left the Yard on horseback to the boos and jeers from the crowd.

The spectacle was over so the people dispersed. Three soldiers remained on guard at the scaffold. A small number of plainly dressed individuals remained in close proximity to the prisoners and offered encouraging words. Bastwick's wife knelt by the scaffold and wept quietly.

Henry stood off in the distance and tried to decide what to do. He wanted to console Bastwick's wife, but feared he would be arrested if he drew close to the scaffold. Archbishop Laud was already suspicious of him and his connection with Dr. Bastwick. He studied Bastwick's wife for a moment. She had always been so kind to him and he hated to see her so distraught, but what could he do to help. Finally, Henry retreated to a bench in front of a shop where he could view the scene unnoticed.

A few moments later, a horse galloped toward the scaffold. The executioner dismounted and with a scowl on his face flew up the steps of the ladder to the platform. He drew his sword and hacked off the rest of Bastwick's ear. A massive amount of blood and another portion of Bastwick's ear fell on the platform. The executioner spat on the blood and piece of ear. Then he clamored down the ladder, mounted his horse and rode away.

Astonished by the executioner's reappearance, Henry whispered to a man standing near him. "What do you think provoked that?"

"I heard that Archbishop Laud had spies in the crowd. And he wasn't happy with the executioner's service. Laud ordered him to return and complete the job on Bastwick's ear. Laud's never happy with anything these days, including brutality. Join me in a pint of ale? I'm tired of watching this travesty."

Henry glanced at Bastwick's wife and said, "Nay, I think I'll wait here awhile."

"Suit yeself," the man said and left.

Two boys equipped with a stash of rocks, rotten vegetables and manure, began pelting the men. Bastwick, Pyrnne and Burton's heads were so tightly bound in the stocks that they could not move to avoid the items thrown at them.

"Good-un John!" yelled on of the boys as a tomato splattered above Reverend Burton's right eye.

The other boy laughed as he grabbed a huge rock. "Watch, this-un! I'll tear the top of his head off."

All at once, a gigantic red-haired man with strong muscular arms, and a long red beard stomped over to the boys. He grabbed each by an arm and bellowed,"Ya boys get out of here now or I'll break both of ya arms!"

"But we won't get our coins!" cried one boy.

"What coins?" the red-haired man asked.

"The coins from that man."

Henry looked in the direction the boy pointed. He saw a distant cleric on a street corner retreating from the scene.

"Well, ye don't deserve coins from the likes of him, especially harming good men as these. Now leave before ye lose the use of ya arms."

The boys walked away, muttering to themselves.

The day wore on and the hot sun bore down on the three men on the platform. Henry stood on a side corner, but he remained in the shadows. Mrs. Bastwick remained by the scaffold. She offered encouragement to her husband whenever the guards were distracted. Occasionally, a wandering boy threw a stone or rotten vegetable at the men, but all immediately admonished by adults nearby. The three men continued to defend their faith to all who would listen throughout the long ordeal.

In the early afternoon, Henry overheard a conversation between two bystanders.

"Did ye hear that Archbishop Laud 'tis disturbed by their talk?" one man said as he pointed to the three men on the scaffold.

"Well, how's he plan to stop it. Cut out their tongues?"

"I wouldn't be surprised. I heard he made a motion to the Lords who are now sitting in the Star Chamber to gag Pyrnne or have some censure on them."

As the rumor spread, people began to congregate around the men. They anticipated more excitement. Henry remained on the side street silently willing the extreme punishment to end. Word finally came that Laud's motion to the Lords had not succeeded. Murmurings and rumors continued circulating among the people throughout the rest of the day. The prisoners were finally removed from the scaffold around dusk.

As Bastwick descended the platform, he drew from his ear a blood soaked sponge, and raised it to the remaining stragglers around as he spoke. "Blessed be my God who hath counted me worthy and enabled me to suffer for his sake; and as now I have lost some of my blood, so I am ready to spill every drop in the veins for this cause for which I now have suffered, which is for maintaining the truth of God, and the honor of my King against popish usurpation. Let God be glorified and the King live forever."

His words, stirred those assembled around the scaffold and they cheered approval. Soon others joined the group. The soldier guarding Bastwick grabbed Bastwick's arm and pushed him down the ladder. He tumbled to the ground. The soldiers on the ground pulled Bastwick to the waiting cart and chained his arms to the sides. One stuffed a cloth in his mouth.

Prynne and Burton were released from the scaffold. Both men appeared faint so offered no remarks. They were led down to the waiting cart and chained to the sides. The cart creaked slowly away from the New Palace Yard. The remaining assemblage of people watched with sadness as the cart passed. Some looked away. It was hard to look at the gruesome faces and mangled ears of the prisoners.

Henry remained until the cart was no longer visible, then walked away. His face was a mask of frustration.

CHAPTER TWO

March 1, 1638, Gravesend, England

Dr. Henry Pattenden was pacing again. He was painfully thin and Mary, his wife, often chided that he would never gain weight because of his constant pacing. She was probably right, but it was his only way of releasing his tension. Presently, he stopped and shouted up the stairs.

"Are you ready, Mary? The coach will be here soon. We must be at the station by 8:00 or you'll miss it."

In their room upstairs, Mary was uneasy. She never liked being away from her husband, and this was an especially difficult time for both of them. She hated to increase his stress, but so many decisions had been forced on her lately and right now, her mind had gone blank. Crates and trunks filled the small rented room, making it hard to move around or even see what was in each one.

What am I forgetting?

The apprehension she had been experiencing daily had suddenly become overwhelming and now she could not concentrate. Her anxiety about their impending journey kept flooding her mind, and made it difficult for her to focus on the task at hand. Then a terrifying realization penetrated her thoughts and she had to sit on the bed for a moment.

Will this be the last time I see my family, or even England? How will I be able to manage without my family nearby?

Mary thought about her mother with her warmth and constant devotion, and her father with his strong defense of his family that always made Mary feel safe. Even her siblings would be difficult to leave behind.

What am I doing? How can I leave them? Now, I must trust only Henry and we've only known each other a short time. And what will he say when he finds out my secret? Will he be upset? I need to talk to Mum and the sooner the better, but I mustn't keep Henry waiting any longer. Whatever I've forgotten, will just have to stay forgotten. I need to see my Mum.

She stood with renewed resolve and shouted down the staircase, "Henry, the trunk 'tis ready."

Henry climbed the stairs and stood at the door of their room a minute while he looked lovingly at his wife. Her long dark hair was tucked under a white rochet trimmed in lace. A few tendrils had escaped, and now framed her face with soft curls like a halo. Her big gray eyes never failed to enchant him. Even though they were in a hurry; he couldn't resist. He walked over and bent down to give his young wife a quick kiss.

As his lips touched hers, Mary reached up to touch his face. His kind, loving concern for her shone back in his eyes, and she knew her answer. Forcing the fearful anxiety back into a far corner compartment of her mind, Mary exclaimed, "Henry, just think we'll soon start our exciting adventure. Oh, I do love you dear husband."

"And I love you," he replied. "We must be on our way. The coach will not wait." After one last glance around the room, Mary followed her husband down the stairs.

Three days later, Dr. Henry Pattenden stood on the edge of the quay stroking his chin as he stared into the vast emptiness of the water before him. He was gripped by another one of his melancholy moods. The moods were occurring with more frequency and were difficult to overcome when Mary was not around. She was aware of the overwhelming despair her husband suffered and on these occasions, her cheerful disposition often enabled the young bride to tease his dark moods away, but she was not with him now. She was visiting her family and he couldn't shake his state of mind. Mary always found something optimistic about any situation and he needed her happy reassurance now as he struggled with self-doubt.

Am I being foolish? Is this some wild idea that will only bring pain or even death to us both? I know so little about the Colonies.

Though she tried to maintain an enthusiastic attitude as the departure time drew near, Henry was cognizant of Mary's growing concern about leaving. He knew how it felt to be without a family nearby, and he hated to put her through the same pain. He smiled as he recalled the day he first met Mary. He remembered her as a beautiful child with dark gray eyes, and when he returned to claim her as his bride, he'd been amazed at what an attractive young lady she'd become in his absence. The scene unfolded in his mind as if it was yesterday, and he chuckled to himself as he recalled his bold entrance back into her life.

Mary was standing behind her father and looked terrified on the day he arrived unannounced at her home. Yet she still managed to give him a faint smile. She wore a gray linen shift that matched the gray in her large eyes. Her long dark hair was draped around her porcelain face and tied with a simple gray ribbon.

"Young man," her father exclaimed. "Ye are correct. Mary was promised to ye by an agreement thy father and I made some eighteen odd years ago. Our first born were to be wed. But Mary is not even fifteen years and knows ye not."

"A promise is a promise, Mr. Willson," Henry added. "And I am in need of a wife now. I have a trade and plan to start my life."

"Henry, I intend to keep my promise to ya dear departed Papa. Lord knows, he was my closest and dearest friend and I owe him my life, but understand me position. Mary's me first-born. I wish her to be happy. Besides, she still needs more time to learn to become a good wife and ye've been away a long time and not had a proper courtship. Stay a time with us so ye'll know each other better before marrying. I'm sure ye will not regret the wait."

"Aye, you give me cause to ponder. I have land in the Colonies and hoped to set sail in a month. Still as you say, I do need a properly trained wife. How long do you think it will be before she is ready?"

"Who knows?" Mary's father laughed. "Ye'll know when the time is right if ye spend more time with her before marriage."

"I guess you give me no choice—I'll wait. However, I will not be staying here. I have a place to stay and with your approval, I will court Mary."

Henry laughed to himself, as he recalled their subsequent courtship. He was so awkward whenever he tried to talk to Mary and she was also very shy. However, her father was correct. It was worth the wait and when they finally wed, on September 12th, her sixteenth birthday, Henry realized how deeply he had fallen in love with her.

His thoughts returned to their engagement in the spring of 1637. As was the custom, Mary's brother, George, presented her with a beautiful horseshoe he made. Mary's clan tartan ribbon, the Scottish thistle and satin ribbon roses were engraved on it. She wore the horseshoe all summer for good luck but it was quite heavy and Henry chuckled aloud as he recalled a comment Mary made toward the end of summer.

"Henry, we should have the most luck in the world if the weight of this horseshoe means anything! Me thinks George, added extra weight for spite. It would be just like him to do so. But since we'll need considerable good luck in this new land of yours, it's worth the pain."

They decided to wed on her birthday because as she stated, "Surely, you will never forget me birthday and anniversary at the same time and as it's said that when you marry in September's shine, your living will be rich and fine."

Three weeks before the date of their marriage, the wedding banns announced their upcoming nuptials in their church. As was required Mary and Henry did not attend church during those weeks to avoid bad luck.

The day of Henry and Mary's wedding dawned bright and beautiful. Henry remembered the vision of her walking down the aisle in the church in her plain white linen shift, carrying her favorite yellow mums.

"She was truly a beautiful bride," Henry whispered to himself as he continued to reminiscence about their wedding.

The priest took the ring from a pillow and touched the thumb, the first finger, and then the second finger of Mary's hand as he declared, "In the name of the Father, the Son, and the Holy Ghost." He placed the ring on Mary's third finger and said, "Amen."

The priest repeated the same with Henry's ring. Then came the magical moment when Henry and Mary first kissed as man and wife.

As they left the church, all their friends and family showered her head with wheat. Henry chuckled to himself as he recalled the expression on Mary's face when she forgot to duck and wheat flew in her eye, blinding her for a moment. She laughed as Henry managed to catch her before she fell down the church steps.

How I miss your laughter. I can't wait to see you again, sweet Mary!

Even at the age of sixteen, Mary was mature beyond her years, especially after a particularly bad day when death seemed to be everywhere and he knew he was helpless to prevent it.

She is indispensable to me now, but am I being selfish by dragging her to the Colonies with me? Mayhaps, I should go first and send for her when I am settled.

Henry abandoned the idea as soon as it came to mind.

I can not imagine life without her. Why would I want to even try? Still, is this adventure fair to her?

The quay was a busy place but Henry was oblivious to the noise surrounding him until his reverie was broken by a loud shout.

"Well, Halloa!"

Henry glanced down the quay and saw the robust, rosy-cheeked figure of William Berriman, dressed in a red jerkin and leather breeches, advance toward him.

"Never thought I'd see ye here so early this morning." William said. "Not with a pretty bride at home."

"I thought I'd come down and check on the repairs," Henry responded. "Mary's visiting her family. What brings you here?"

Henry liked Berriman. Though he'd only known him for a few days, Berriman proved to be a valuable friend by allowing Henry to store some of his medical supplies in the space Berriman was allotted on the Elizabeth.

"Just checking on repairs, same as ye." replied Berriman as he joined Henry. "'Tis hard to wait and spend me profits on the high rent in town. Have ye heard the sail date yet? I hope it's soon. I need to be on me way now. I've bought ten more indentures to take to Virginia and need to sell them before planting time."

"Why do you sell indentured servants? Don't they help with your planting?"

"I couldn't manage without them. Tried to a few years ago— went bust. But I have all I need now. I just want their headrights. There's always people wanting to go to the Colonies these days and I aim to transport any of them that want to go, in exchange for their headrights."

"Exchange for their headrights?"

"Aye, headrights. As you know, every person traveling to Virginia receives a headright of fifty acres and by paying for others transport in exchange for that headright, I gain a tidy sum of acres with little cost to me. They're also indentured to me for seven years. I can use them to plant and harvest my land or sell them to other needy planters at a handsome profit. Either way, I can't lose." Berriman laughed, "Great system and perfectly legal."

"Sounds like it. Mayhaps I should look into purchasing some indentures. I know I could use the help."

"Ye say ya bride's with her family. She hasn't backed out of traveling to the Colonies, has she?"

"On the contrary, she's anxious to leave. I wanted her to have time to say good-bye to her family without me around. She's trying to talk her parents into following us to the Colonies. She hates to leave them here with all this turmoil in England."

"I know 'tis trying to leave family, still it's for the best. 'Tis not safe here in England, especially with your connection with Bastwick and that atrocity Laud perpetrated on him. Who knows what Laud will do next? Have ye heard where Bastwick was sent?"

"Sicily, I believe. I didn't want to ask too many questions. Laud's already suspicious enough of my connection with Bastwick and has made several queries about me. That's why I feel compelled to leave England as soon as possible."

"Ye be doing the right thing. With me living in Virginia, and traipsing back and forth between here and there, I haven't kept up with things here in England. I thought William Laud was a Protestant. What got him so riled against Bastwick?"

"The whole thing started after Laud, succeeded to the archbishopric of Canterbury on the death of the Abbot. Bastwick printed two treatises in the Netherlands and Laud thought they were targeted at him so he had Bastwick fined, excommunicated and prohibited from practicing medicine. His books were burned and he was imprisoned."

"But writing treatises is hardly enough to have him pilloried, him being a gentleman as well."

"I guess everyone was fooled by Laud. He seems to hold opinions closely aligned with the Pope and is King Charles right-hand in putting down religious liberties. Laud's action only intensified Bastwick's beliefs and he responded with two more books, one written in English, in which he charged that bishops were the enemies of God and the tail of the beast!'."

"Tail of the beast! Strong language. Is that when Laud retaliated with the Star Chamber?"

"Aye, he took Bastwick and two other Puritan activists, William Prynne and Reverend Henry Burton to the Star Chamber where they were prosecuted at the same time. They were censured and condemned to pay a fine of five thousand pounds each. Afterward the men were set in the New Palace Yard, and they suffered the torture of having their ears cut off. In addition to that, they were branded and banished to imprisonment for life in remote parts of the kingdom without access to pen or paper."

"The punishment is unbelievable, particularly since they were honest gentlemen. At least you will be out of Laud's grasp in Virginia."

"True, there's little left for me to do here, though I feel I am betraying Dr. Bastwick. He's an honorable man. Without him, I would not be a surgeon today. After my father died, he took me in and taught me surgery. When he closed his medical practice, I went to the Colonies briefly, and I've not talked with him since then, still there's no telling what Laud might do. Did you hear that he nearly caused a riot at St. Giles in Scotland?"

"Nay, I hadn't heard. What happened?" asked Berriman.

"The Dean of Edinburgh, clad in canonicals, began reading from the new liturgy for worship. Of course, this angered the congregation and they started shouting. Then a young girl, I believe her name was Janet Geddes, actually threw a stool at the Dean."

"Brave lass, this Janet Geddes. What did the Dean do then?"

"He panicked and ran from the room; the Bishop of Edinburgh tried to continue the service, but the people called him a Pope and Antichrist. Both men barely escaped and only with the help of their magistrates. Since then, I heard that the Privy Council of Scotland sent a representative to King Charles to state the feelings of the Scots, but the King has declared all who opposed the new liturgy as traitors."

"Someone told me that King Charles was raising an army. I wondered why. Do ye think he will go against Scotland?"

"Who knows what he'll do next? I only hope Mary's family does not get involved. I really hate to leave them here."

"You are doing the right thing by leaving. Imagine what would happen once Laud discovered ya connection with Bastwick. Think of ya pretty young wife. Would ye want her to go through such torment?"

Henry grimaced as he was reminded of the scene at the pillory when Bastwick's weeping wife retrieved his hacked off ears and held them close to her breast. He knew that scene would be etched in his mind forever.

The thought of putting Mary through such a horrible ordeal was something I could never face. It will be safer for us in the Colonies.

"How does ya young bride feel about traveling to Virginia?"

"She's anxious to be on our way, yet worried. Mary fears for her parents' safety. I wish they'd agree to follow us there. They're determined to stay in England. I know life will be difficult for Mary in Virginia without them. My brief visit there assured me of that."

"Aye, that is true, but 'tis far enough away from Laud and all his ordinances and that is worth more. So ye've been to Virginia? When were ye there?"

"As I said, I studied under Dr. Bastwick. After he stopped treating the sick and began writing, I left him for a time and hired on as the surgeon on a trip to Virginia. I stayed about a year in Jamestown and acquired 200 acres through headrights. I haven't patented the land yet since I was not sure where I want to settle. I returned to England about a year ago to wed Mary, in time to witness Bastwick being pilloried."

"Ya said ye have 200 acres. Have you decided where you want to settle?"

"At first, I thought about Jamestown. However, Mary has an uncle in Accawmacke and he encouraged us to settle there. We plan to stay with him for awhile after we reach Virginia."

"Accawmacke, ya say, why that's where I have my plantation! What's Mary's uncle's name?"

"Henry Willson, do you know him?"

"Ye wife's uncle is Henry Willson? Why of course I know Henry! He married me Mum in England after me father died. He left for Virginia with his bother John and sent for us after things were a little more settled. I was around nineteen when we first arrived in Virginia and I remember how shocked I was by the primitive conditions at the time in Virginia."

"That must be him. He settled in Virginia quite awhile back. Are there many young women in the Colonies?"

"Not enough, especially around me. I have my wife, Sarah, and my sister-in-law, Elizabeth, and of course, me Mum. Elizabeth married Henry Carsley, Jr., me stepbrother from Mum's first marriage. I've been helping Elizabeth some after her husband died a couple of years ago and she has two daughters Agnis, and Francis."

"Where does Henry Willson live in Accawmacke?"

"Henry and me Mum live on Old Plantation Creek. I believe he's one of the oldest planters in Accawmacke that is still alive. He arrived around twenty years ago. Henry Willson helped set up the salt mines on Smith Island when Accawmacke was first settled. A better man can not be found."

"Salt mines. Is there salt in Accawmacke?"

Berriman laughed, "Of course, there's salt, a whole ocean full. If they had not set up the salt works to secure salt by evaporation from the ocean, Virginia may never have been settled. There was no other way to preserve meat and we wouldn't have survived long with just fresh meat. The salt works were set up by Sir Thomas Dale around 1614, I believe, but Henry Willson's group really made the salt works profitable."

"I see, but evaporation seems to be a very hard way to make salt."

"True, it was, until old man Mile Pirket came to Virginia to manage the works. Somehow he and a few other men managed to make a profit. When Henry Willson went to Accawmacke to help with the salt works, he said he fell in love with the eastern shore and stayed. Since ye have so many relatives in Accawmacke, ya ought to settle there. Ye could do worse."

"Well that would be good for Mary. It would be nice to be near relatives, even ones she doesn't know well."

"We're seldom bothered by Jamestown courts since 'tis a ways across the bay which is good for ye. The further from Laud's hooks the better, I'd say. Jamestown receives orders from England that we sometimes ignore in Accawmacke. Though I won't deceive ya, there are tough times ahead. But in Accawmacke a man can build a good life—that is if he's willing to work."

"I'm not afraid of work. I only hope it won't be too difficult for

Mary. She's heard many stories about the savages, and I'm afraid they've terrified her. Is it true that the Indians are friendly in Accawmacke? Her uncle wrote us that they've never had trouble with them."

"Aye, they're friendly in my part of the woods. Still, I wouldn't turn me back on them. We've never had anything like the savagery perpetrated on the people in Jamestown. Why they say, before that massacre on the western shore in 1622, Devedeavon, or the Laughing King as he's called, warned of the uprising and his warning saved Jamestown from total devastation. Everyone was able to prepare with guns and ammunition. We owe a lot to the Laughing King on Accawmacke. The land, however, is worth any tribulation. The soil's so fertile and the weather so mild that I've produced two crops each year since I've been there. And there are no stones to break a plough. The forests are filled with wildlife and there's all manner of fish or shellfish just for the taking. I'd say it's a paradise and I can't wait to get back."

"Well, you certainly make Accawmacke sound appealing."

"Why don't ye and Mary come stay with me and Sarah a spell when we reach Virginia and see for yourself?"

"That's a very kind offer. Of course, we plan to stay with Mary's uncle first."

"Sarah will enjoy visiting with ya missus. She gets a mite lonely for womanly company."

A loud racket down the quay startled Henry and Berriman. They looked in the direction of the sound and saw soldiers racing toward them. Henry was alarmed as they drew near. He gave a sigh of relief as they ran past them and went further down the quay.

Henry and Berriman watched a man untying a skiff. He glanced up and saw the soldiers. His fearful eyes darted around for some means of escape, and seeing none, he jumped into the water. Two soldiers dived in after him. They struggled with the man briefly before finally subduing him. Then they heaved the man out of the water and onto the deck. His hands were quickly bound behind his back. Two soldiers held him by his arms and pulled him down the quay. Henry and Berriman overheard the man repeating, "I can do all things through Christ, who strengtheneth me," over and over again as they passed.

William looked at Henry and remarked, "I'd say the Elizabeth won't be leaving any too soon for either of us."

Buy full version of Ribbon of Love

at

Amazon.com

or

Barnes and Noble

ISBN: 978-1508807353
Soft cover edition

ASIN: B005LIX4PE
Kindle Edition

TAPESTRY OF LOVE SERIES

RIBBON OF LOVE – Book one

FAITH AND COURAGE - Book two

FREEHEARTS – Book Three

New Series

THE COTTINGHAMS

DISCORDANCE – Book One

Additional Books by Donna R. Causey can be found on her websites

www.alabamapioneers.com

www.daysgoneby.me

Follow Donna R. Causey on FACEBOOK

http://www.facebook.com/ribbonoflove

and contact her via her

Author's Page on Amazon.com

Printed in Great Britain
by Amazon